Salvatore Santagati
A First Spring in Sicily

Maria SS. Addolorata
An old Sicilian image representing the Passion. It used to be found on
the rustic walls of many country families,
especially at Easter time.

Salvatore Santagati
A First Spring in Sicily

IN MEMORIAM
B.A.J. (1939-1990)

Thine absence overflows the rose
From every petal gleam

Such words as it were vain to close,
Such tears as crowd the dream.

Hart Crane

A Paperback Original
*
Almond Grove Press
London

Contents

I

Stories

II

Poems

III

A Literary Screenplay

Front cover illustration : Vergine annunciata (1474)
by Antonello da Messina, Palermo, Sicily.

I
Stories

Maria's Chrysanthemums

I

Since her husband had died earlier in the year a gradual transformation seemed to have taken place in Maria's life.

As was customary in her native Sicilian village, Maria's marriage had been arranged by her parents.

On her marriage she had just reached the age of seventeen.

She had then a graceful, ivory figure, large black eyes, and her beautiful black hair almost touched her knees.

The expression on her face had the pure, melancholy innocence of one of Antonello da Messina's Sicilian Madonnas.

Maria had been born to a family of small farmers. Her family had lived a simple and untroubled existence at the edge of their village which lay between two hills.

A large baroque church stood on top of one of the hills.

On clear days the sea could be seen in the far distance, reflecting the blue of the sky.

At the centre of their house there was a spacious courtyard shaded all year round by an orange tree.

During springtime, when the orange tree was in full flower, the air was sweet with the scent of blossom.

II

The courtyard was the focus of much human as well as animal life.

There her mother reared chickens, pigeons, rabbits and a few turkeys. The house was full of their pleasing noises. The crumbling walls of the courtyard were covered with drying oregano, garlic, onions and basil.

The house, being at the edge of the village, overlooked the silver of the olive orchards, and further afield there were hills and valleys with dried streams. Their slopes were covered in vineyards, almond trees and fields of artichokes.

Their house also had a terrace lined with large pots of delicately scented basil, rosemary and geraniums.

On the terrace the children often played and occasionally broke some of the pots.

When they broke a pot their mother would scream at them, a scream which the children knew was no more than a mild reproach.

Maria's mother kept herself busy all day long with the children, the house, the animals, the preparation of meals; while her husband went out every morning, before dawn, riding on his mule to the family's plot of land, a one-and -a-half hour ride away, along many narrow stony tracks.

Maria's oldest sister, Concetta, helped the family by working daily in her room doing embroidery for other families in the village, who were preparing the dowries for their daughters' future marriages.

In later years Maria helped her sister Concetta with her embroidery.

III

The husband whom her parents had chosen for Maria was, naturally, from the same background for in her village the classes rarely mixed.

In Sicilian his name was Totò, although on his birth certificate and other official documents he was known as Salvatore.

He was the son of a small farmer and worked a plot of land next to that of Maria's father.

When Totò had finished the compulsory elementary school, his father took him every dawn to work with him on the land. His continual exposure to the sun made his body permanently tanned and the tip of his nose was almost always flaking.

When he and Maria married, his family bought him a plot of land. There, conscientiously, he cultivated wheat, vegetables and fruits for his family.

Maria's sister (who for no particular reason had not married) embroidered her sister a dowry: linen with pretty patterns in pink, towels, pillow-cases, tea towels and curtains. She even prepared some baby clothes.

IV

Early in their married life Maria had given birth to five children, three boys and two girls, and she had led a busy untroubled existence for all these years.

She adored her husband and had enjoyed looking after the children.

The oldest of the boys had decided to follow the example of some of his school friends, abandoning the land of their fathers, and had migrated to the north of Italy.

There, he had found for himself a job as a waiter in a bar. He was happy living in a big city and came back to see his family once a year in August.

Before falling asleep at night Maria made the sign of the cross and in her whispered prayers often thanked the Lord for having given her such a good, hard-working husband who was neither drunk nor violent, as many men were in the village.

Even the children had rarely given cause for worry. Maria had good relations with her neighbours and never interfered in their personal lives.

V

For many years after their marriage Maria's husband, like her father, had gone out to work on his land every morning, before dawn and in all seasons.

In the evenings the hard-wearing bags over his mule were full of produce for the family: oranges, lemons, olives, almonds, onions, wild asparagus (which he laboriously retrieved from their thorny bushes) and wild vegetables like the Sicilian bitter "cicoria" which Maria cooked with pasta in the evenings.

Twice a week, on Saturdays and on Sundays, she killed a couple of chickens or rabbits, filled them with rosemary and black olives, and roasted them on the breezy terrace, while the children played excitedly around the fire.

Once a fortnight she made the bread for the whole family which lasted them for two weeks. During these two weeks the bread never seemed to become stale.

On these occasions she got up in the middle of the night, for the preparations were laborious and lengthy.

Especially during the winter months, when it was pleasant to be in front of an oven heated by hard almond shells, the baking turned into a festive event.

Maria treated the whole family to hot pizzas, garlic and olive breads, roasted turkey with rosemary, and baked potatoes with aromatic herbs which they all loved.

VI

At Eastertime she prepared bread in the form of doves with an egg in the centre and a variety of Easter sweets.

When the summer arrived, there was always an abundance of tomatoes.

As was traditional in her part of Sicily, she cut the tomatoes in half, placed them on long wooden boards, salted them and then placed these boards on the terrace and on the roof of the house.

Since many of the other women in the village made the same preparations, from the church's steps there was a sea of red covering the rooftops.

Within a few days the hot sun dried the tomatoes.

Maria made little sandwiches of the dried tomatoes, filling them with fresh basil and garlic.

She then placed the dried tomatoes neatly in glass jars, filled the jars with thick, green olive oil and left them to marinate.

These and other delicacies served as quick snacks for the family.

VII

As the years went by, Maria began to plait her long, black hair and started to gather it in a large knot behind her head.

Once a week she released her hair and washed it under running water near the stable.

Then she sat on a chair and spent a good hour in the sunshine continually combing and drying it. Her face was barely visible.

Her ivory figure had changed and, by the time she reached the age of thirty, she looked just like many other housewives in her village.

In the early evening as her husband was about to approach the village she often took her youngest child and went out to meet him.

On seeing them approach her husband dismounted from the mule, then he put the boy on top of the mule, and Maria and her husband walked happily towards home.

VIII

In later years, following the example of other farmers, Maria's husband decided to buy a Vespa motor scooter, which had been designed for small farmers.

This meant that he could cut the journey to work by half and make use of the new tarmac roads.

When he reached the point closest to his land he had to ride it for about two kilometres along a stony and uneven track.

One late afternoon when he had finished his day's work he packed his linen bag with small blood oranges, a reserve of which he kept in his wooden shed under the large fig tree, and set off for home.

It was a day in July, in the early sixties.

While riding over the uneven track, that late summer afternoon, Maria's husband hit a rugged stone. His Vespa went out of control and he fell, hitting his head against another stone.

As he fell to the ground the oranges came rolling out of his bag.

Then, effortlessly, he lifted himself, picked up the spilled oranges one by one, leaving the fractured ones on the ground.

With his hands he touched his temples.

In the palm of his right hand he noticed some traces of dark red blood, shining under the sun's light.

His gaze then turned towards the stone. It too was stained with the same velvety blood.

At that very moment, and before he could realise the gravity of what had happened, Maria's beloved husband lost consciousness and his body fell once again on the stony, uneven track.

The little blood oranges came rolling out for the second time. Some of them rolled into the ditch. Others, a few of which on impact began bleeding, came to rest around his bleeding head.

A trickling stream of blood had reached his unshaven chin.

His body stayed there, motionless.

His eyes were gently closed.

His black cap lay close to his shoulders, revealing his sandy, golden brown hair.

His thick, corduroy trousers were torn close to the knee.

The sun had begun to lose its strength, while the surrounding countryside was starting to relish the gentle, cooling glow of sunset.

IX

Some time later a farmer passed by, riding a mule. But by the time he had raised the alarm, and the nearest hospital had been reached, Maria's husband had entered a coma.

He died two days later without ever re-opening his eyes.

Heartbroken and weeping Maria kissed his still warm forehead and held his hand for a while.

She felt a cold stream passing through his body.

Then she went out of the room to call the doctors.

A nurse covered his head with the white, crisp fold of the top sheet and then accompanied Maria to her relatives waiting outside in the long shiny corridors.

It happened in the early evening as people in the piazza were starting to gather for the evening passeggiata and where the news of the death of Maria's husband would spread in no time.

Two days later black-edged notices appeared on the white, rustic walls of the village.

At the funeral of her husband, Maria had been emotional, but this was not in any way different from most other funerals which took place in her village. (In many Sicilian funerals it is a social requirement to be extreme in the public expression of grief, whether or not the grief is genuinely felt.)

After a few months had passed, however, Maria's grief was having a strange effect on her otherwise orderly personality.

She had naturally complied with all the outward requirements of Sicilian bereavement by wearing black — black clothes, black stockings and black shoes.

She felt her mourning was permanent and so she burnt all her coloured clothes.

Then she suddenly ceased to visit her relatives.
She started to ignore her children.

The focus of her daily life became centred around the dawn pilgrimages which she made to her husband's grave.
Every morning she brought him fresh flowers which she placed below his studio photograph.

Her grief began to take other directions.

X

In all weathers she went out covered in a big black shawl to the local shops without stopping or speaking to anyone.

On Sunday mornings while Mass was being celebrated she sat, alone, at the back.

Several months after the death of her husband, Maria began to grow suspicious of her relatives, her neighbours and the village priest.

She became convinced that they were all conspiring to isolate her from the rest of the community because she showed signs of being available to the men in the congregation.

She started to suspect that the priest who had conducted her husband's funeral was starting to take advantage of her vulnerability by making passes at her during mass.

When she saw her neighbours coming out of their houses, she shouted and insulted them.

They began to be afraid of her accusations. The neighbours avoided passing in front of her house, whose front door was permanently draped in black.

This confirmed her suspicions of the conspiracy going on around her.

XI

One Sunday, in the middle of the morning mass, when the Church was filled with village people including many of the local dignitaries, Maria stormed into the church.

She climbed on to the altar.

Then, standing on the ornate altar, to the astonishment of the priest in his golden, embroidered robes below and the congregation before her, Maria started shouting her accusations of the conspiracy against her.

How the priest had tried to seduce her.

How her neighbours refused to pass in front of her house.

How her children had turned against her.

How her relatives had shunned her.

Sobbing, she then lay face down on the altar.

On touching the cold marble of the altar, a chill current passed through her body.

The richly patterned, gold-plated chalice came falling down the steps, making a sharp metallic sound inside the church.

Amplified by the acoustics of the large white and sky-blue dome, her cries reverberated throughout the building, brilliant in the morning light.

XII

Then November came, and brought the feast of All Souls, the first after the death of her husband.

Maria had by then become more tranquil and, like all the other people in her village who had lost their loved ones, she made preparations to pay particular respect to her husband by ornamenting his black marble grave with new winter flowers and branches from flowering shrubs.

Early on the morning of All Souls' Day Maria descended towards the cemetery, which was situated at the edge of the village.

The funeral route was lined with tall, slim cypress trees.

At the entrance to the cemetery the route would become crowded with hundreds of mourners, the women mostly in black, the men wearing their best Sunday suits and black ties.

In the lapels of their jackets they had either a black button or a black silk stripe.

Between the cypress trees there would be many flower vendors selling the most beautiful globed chrysanthemums whose dazzling yellows and russets seemed to glow.

They also sold dark mourning roses and branches from rare black-berried shrubs.

Some of the vendors sold black balloons for the children and many varieties of seeds and nuts for everybody to eat during the whole day they were to spend at the gravesides.

Many of the men carried portable radios and the women carried baskets covered in golden straw containing food for the graveside picnics.

Some women, whose wounds of a recent bereavement were still raw, came supported by relatives.

On that fine November morning, Maria arrived at her husband's grave as most other mourners were preparing to leave their houses.

She wore her large black shawl, and in her arms she bore a big cluster of yellow chrysanthemums.

Once in front of her husband's grave, Maria arranged the flowers neatly on the cold, black marble.

When she had finished arranging the yellow flowers, she knelt down and kissed the old tombstone photograph which had been taken at the time of their marriage.

Then, calmly, she undressed herself and, naked, she lay amid the brilliant colours of the yellow chrysanthemums, gazing up at the fresh, blue November sky.

*

First broadcast in 1990 on BBC Radio 3 during the interval of a promenade concert. It was broadcast again on Radio 3 in 1991. The reader was Robert Rietty.

*

There, Under the Patchy Shadow of an Almond Tree

I

During springtime Francesco's town is at its most beautiful.

Lying stretched on a breezy ridge, it commands vast views into the barren, sun-burned heart of Sicily.

Its slopes, covered with ancient olive groves and almond trees in full blossom, descend to join the golden wheatfields below, sprinkled with luxurious red poppies.

The occasional gust of wind sends the whole landscape into sweet motion.

The air becomes filled with countless white petals blown off the almond trees.

The surrounding hills, in a dazzling light, are covered in square patches of purple, yellow, red and white wild flowers.

At one end of Francesco's town, perched on an adjoining hill, lies a Norman castle, its main tower still standing.

There, during afternoons when the town is at its most sleepy, he often goes to look at the distant views, while letting his mind run free.

At the other end of the town a decaying baroque palace faces a battered, tired-looking council estate, with long lines of drying clothes, tomatoes and aromatic herbs.

Francesco lives near the council estate in an old cottage with enormously thick walls.

II

It is the late fifties and Francesco is a fifteen year old boy studying at a technical college in a larger town by the sea.

Particularly during springtime, he enjoys getting up at five-thirty every morning. Then, he quickly splashes his body with cold water which he has poured into a metal bowl and rushes to the junction of the town's Corso to catch his bus at six.

He finds the one-and-a-half-hour journey to college very beautiful. He observes, in motion, and with fascination, the singular birth of each day and its soft blend of coloured lights.

By the time he arrives to attend classes at eight Francesco feels both refreshed and alert.

At one o'clock, his classes finished, he regularly spends about an hour by the sea. The heat drives him to the nearest secluded sand dunes.

There, he strips himself naked, and runs on the burning sands, plunging his firm olive-coloured body into the salty waters of the sea.

In the far distance a huge oil refinery, resembling a metallic futurist city, looks on.

Then, with his shoulders against the hot sun, he contentedly eats the lunch which he has himself prepared the night before — a chunk of home-made bread, a piece of black-peppered cheese, salted black olives, a couple of earthy tomatoes and a large blood orange.

By two-thirty he is punctually waiting to catch his bus home. During the journey back, exhausted by the afternoon heat, he often falls into an uncomfortable sleep.

III

One day, after having eaten his lunch, with his body still on the soft sand, he falls into a deep and dreamy sleep and misses his bus back home.

After waking up he decides to spend the rest of the afternoon by the sea, reading and enjoying the relaxing sound of the waves.

Late in the afternoon, when the heat has become less intense, Francesco begins walking towards home.

And when the occasional car passes by, he makes a discreet sign for a lift. He is not really worried if nobody stops, for he is thoroughly enjoying strolling along the semi-deserted country roads.

But, after about an hour, a man driving a white car stops to offer him a lift home.

To Francesco he looks a kind and lively man. His brilliant white teeth, when he smiles, provide a stark contrast to his handsome, dark brown face.

A married man with two young children, he works as a bank manager in the town where Francesco goes to college.

He lives in a large modern town house with intricately

patterned gates and also owns a baroque villa in the surrounding hills.

There, in the baroque villa, in the evenings and at weekends, he likes to work in his garden and lemon orchard.

He is particularly proud of his garden where he has grown some exotic plants, plants which he has brought back from his travels in the not-too-distant Africa.

During the hot summer months he moves his family to stay in his old country villa.

In the coolness of the early evenings hours, under a huge carob tree, he enjoys preparing imaginative barbecues with spicy sausages, pieces of marinated meats, artichokes and salted black olives which the whole family then eats, accompanied by garden salads and local fruity red wines.

He is a really contented man.

A spontaneous and immediate fondness blossoms between Francesco and this contented man.

They soon learn a lot about each other's lives and they realise that their minds, as well as their bodies, are truly attracted to each other.

And it is Francesco who, on seeing the approach of sunset, asks his new friend to stop on a small track looking across a valley.

There, under the patchy shadow of an almond tree, they know the sweetest of love.

IV

During subsequent weeks they become closer and closer.

After work the man often collects Francesco from his home and together they go to his villa. There, Francesco helps him in the garden.

At weekends they go hunting.

Not that Francesco enjoys the killing of wild animals. He goes hunting in order to spend as much time as possible with his friend.

Indeed one day when he is about to shoot a beautiful red fox, Francesco alarms his friend by placing himself in front of him, thus preventing the beautiful red fox from being killed.

Francesco's courage touches his friend so much that for some weeks after the event, during the early evening passeggiata when the Corso is filled with men, he keeps retelling the story to his friends.

Francesco's happiness, however, often turns as sour as the taste of unripe olives every time the moment of separation arrives.

V

One mid-afternoon, on coming back from college, he overhears a group of old women in black saying that there has been a serious car accident in the hills near the town.

Without any further knowledge Francesco is seized by a ghastly presentiment.

His body begins trembling.
His face turns red hot.
His breathing becomes jerky.

His heart starts pounding...

And his body begins running in the direction of his
friend's house, along the town's desolate Corso,

lined with old churches,
the occasional group of tired,
unshaven,
seated old men,
in heavy corduroy trousers,
black caps,
and sleeping under the protecting
shadow of a palm tree.

On reaching the intricately patterned gates of his
friend's house he hears the faint cries of women.

He rushes inside the house.

There, in a sparsely furnished room, darkened by
closed venetian shutters, he finds a group of weeping old
women, seated in a half-circle, their heads covered by
long, silky black shawls, comforting a distressed younger
woman.
The silky black shawl makes the younger woman's
face barely visible. In her hands she holds a red
handkerchief with which she often wipes and covers her
face.

On noticing the boy's timid presence by the door,
she raises her head,
and with her large, dark brown eyes,
gives Francesco a fierce —

Almost evil look.

*

A First Spring in Sicily

I

There are two springs in Sicily. The first spring begins in early April when the warm North African breezes start to blow over the island, when the landscape is green and the soil moist from the recent winter rains.

The sea and the sky have a shining beauty while the air is mild and fragrant.

During the first spring a profusion of wild flowers bursts from the soft earth to colour the landscape with shades of yellow, purple and white.

The spring breezes blow crested waves over green meadows.

The roadsides are full of wild flowers — lilies, orchids, corn-marigolds, poppies, white daisies and flowering thistles.

On moorlands and on mountain slopes the air is scented by the wind shaking the flowering mints.

The snow on the higher slopes of Mount Etna is closer to its smoky crater, revealing a network of black lanes of frozen lava which were once incandescent rapids of fire.

Sometimes clumps of mountain flowers can be seen growing in the crevices of the frozen lava.

Almond trees thrive on the lower slopes of Mount Etna where the volcanic soil is dark in richness. During the first spring almond trees bud and burst into flower. The white of the almond blossom then replaces the white of the retreating snow. At times the two whites merge into one and it is possible to see a lost almond tree flowering on a mountain slope covered with snow.

(A magnolia in bloom can also sometimes be seen standing in the snow, its delicate pink-white flowers shining on bare, leafless branches.)

The huge crater of the volcano watches over the whole island spread below its feet. From the summit one suddenly forgets all the changes that have taken place in the human landscape over thousands of years.

In the countryside the fresh air buzzes with many flying insects. At night countless stars can be seen in the deep, black skies while closer to the ground clusters of glow-worms form miniature constellations.

Then by early in July the lion's breath from Africa begins to reach the southern shores of the island, transforming the flowering landscape into dust.

The heat dries up the valley streams and the baked, cracked soil becomes as hard as cement. The desert-like barrenness transforms the once flowering landscape of the first spring into a distant dream — a dream rolling in the heat-haze of the lion's breath.

The second spring of Sicily comes early in November, as the summer months come to a close. It begins with the first winter rains which moisten the hardened, rain-touched landscape. The earth begins to soften and new shoots of green grass appear everywhere in the countryside.

Then out of the newly moistened earth another spring arises.

Mayflowers reappear in December.

The new winter flowers mix harmoniously with the flowers of the first spring and the countryside is once again joyous with the sound and colours of a second spring.

Flights of birds begin to arrive, escaping the cold, darkening winter climates of Northern Europe. They are on their way to Africa and come to rest on the gentle shores of Sicily, enjoying gliding in the warm November air.

This is the record of a journey.

A journey both real and imaginary.

A journey which takes place during a first spring in Sicily.

II

It was early in May, in London in 1989, when a telephone call awoke me from my confused, dreamy sleep. The electronic voice at the other end of the line said: "This is your British Telecom alarm call. It is now 5:25. Thank you for using the services of British Telecom. ... This is your British Telecom alarm call. It is now 5:26. Thank you for using the services of British Telecom. This is...".

Before the message could be repeated a third time I put the phone down. I lingered in bed for a few more minutes. Then at 5:35 the radio alarm turned itself on. I got up. With my eyes half-closed I opened wide the curtains and looked into the garden.

The first of the spring roses were covered with dew drops. The daffodils at the edge of the lawn glowed in the low morning light. The murky-grey sky touched the leaves of the horse-chestnut at the end of the garden, the sound of spring birds could be heard through the damp, misty air.

That night, I had hardly slept.
I felt tired.
My body ached.
My limbs felt like those of an old man.
My grieving heart was dark as night.
I had fallen asleep out of exhaustion.
I had wanted to get away, get away for some time.
I shaved. I showered. I dressed, quickly.
I closed the doors inside the house.
During the night I had packed a few of my belongings — my camera, a pair of corduroy trousers, a few unironed shirts, a blank notebook.

In my wallet I had a piece of paper with the name and phone number of a Sicilian woman given to me a few days earlier by a friend in London.

I checked once again that both my passport and the plane ticket were in my jacket.

My half-filled black case stood ready by the front door. As I walked up and down the stairs I could feel the cold morning air coming in from the streets.

I went out into the drizzling rain. I walked quickly through the amber-lighted streets towards the bus stop. I had to be at the railway station by 6.25, the time when my train would be leaving for Luton Airport.

That May morning the light had difficulty in filtering through the grey clouds. The streets were deserted. The city looked tired. It had an air of weariness, as if it knew that it would soon be ravaged by yet another day's traffic and crowds.

The empty streets and the expectation of travel seemed to have cleared my dark mood. I felt suddenly alert. In two hours I would be flying above that granite sky.

At the bus stop I waited, alone. Ten minutes later, through the mist and the fine spring rain, I saw in the distance the red bus approaching. As it got closer, I waved at the bus driver to make sure he'd see me.

Sitting in the lower deck there was a large, unsmiling woman. She was fortyish and wore a bright yellow raincoat. Her fuzzy red hair was oily wet. As I boarded the bus, neither she nor the conductor looked at me.

Inside, a cold silence.

The conductor sat close to the entrance, huddled in the corner of the long seat. He was a black man in his fifties, a thin, frail man. I could not see his eyes; for he wore a pair of dark glasses held together by dirty tape.

I climbed the stairs and went to sit up front. The bus was empty, cigarettes stubs everywhere and the air was trapped and stale. I opened a few of the windows.

A few moments later, with his ticket machine strapped around his neck and shoulders, the conductor came upstairs to collect my fare. As I gave him the money my right hand touched his dry and icy cold hand.

I was then left alone, alone.

The bus moved through the empty, damp streets.

As we approached King's Cross station I saw a lonely figure trying vainly to sweep the rubbish from the pavements. As he went along he left most of the rubbish on the pavement.

There were the soggy remains of fish and chips, half-eaten kebabs, soiled paper and boxes from the fast-food places which had stayed open until the last trickle of business had dried up. There were also piles of torn black sacks overflowing with the remains from the closed restaurants.

As the bus stopped at a light, in one corner, opposite a restaurant, I saw two emaciated black dogs tearing apart some of the rubbish bags. One of them pulled out a large bone with shreds of dirty, raw flesh.

The other dog pulled out the head of a sheep, still dripping with blood. With his mouth he first pulled out and then ate its brain while the other dog was struggling to have its share. With his paws he then tore out the sheep's soiled eyes and left them on the wet pavement.

At St Pancras I got out of the bus and crossed the traffic-free road. As I walked towards the station the doorways were full of human bodies wrapped in cardboard boxes with the names of luxury department stores printed on them.

I saw a man, with a bewildered expression on his face, whose head was resting on a black rubbish bag. He wore neither shoes nor socks and his feet were badly swollen.

A vomiting sick dog hovered around him.

Close by there was a large tree, leafless and bare. The branches, blackened by the traffic fumes, had dirty plastic bags entangled in them and were moving in the slight morning wind.

As I entered the station, a woman came towards me. My heart shrank.

She had red eyes. Her English-grey hair was tangled and dirty. She was pushing a supermarket trolley full of her belongings — plastic bags filled with old clothes, remains of foods picked up from the streets. Chained to her trolley was a thin, bony cat with desperate eyes.

She asked, in a coarse voice, if I could give her money to buy breakfast in the café. I searched my pocket and gave her the few pound coins I had left.

Her smile touched me, deeply.

For a few moments I thought I was in the middle of a nightmare.

Had I really woken up? Was I still lying in my bed in that dreamy sleep?

I rushed to the ticket office. It was closed. I looked at the empty station. I saw a few thin, dark figures roaming in the large empty space of the station.

A few minutes later the first commuter train arrived. As the doors swung open, waves of pale, anonymous pinstriped figures poured out of the carriages, all carrying umbrellas.

I looked at my watch. It was 6.20. My train would be leaving in exactly five minutes time. I ran towards the platform and got into the first carriage.

Inside there was a young black woman with huge, gleaming eyes. As the train began to move slowly she looked, absently,

   at the rusty, wet rails,
   at the thin morning rain,
   at the trains running past the window,
   at the suburban houses with their dull green patches...

Then my gaze turned inwards.

I felt a strange sense of calm happiness.

I thought of what I had seen. Of leaving behind a brutal, soul-destroying city. A city inhabited by dark shadows.

A city with a rusty-iron soul.

A sick city with a vile sky.

Then … I closed my eyes and slept.

I was wakened by the black woman who sat at the opposite end of the carriage. She shook me with her hand and said quietly "We're in Luton. We're in Luton."

I looked at my watch: it was 7.45. My plane was due to depart at 8.25. As I entered the airport lobby I was surprised to see the place crowded with people.

There were long queues at most of the checkouts. The people were all English.

As I mixed with the crowds I felt a sense of uneasiness. The atmosphere in the airport was like that of an English football match.

It was charged. I felt threatened by the tension and noise around me. I thought a riot was about to break out at any time. A bloody riot like the ones I had seen on television.

I saw men and women at the bookstalls buying books with large, gold-lettered covers. Thuggish young men with greasy hair gazed at lurid newspapers headlines. Others looked at pictures of naked girls. Some children were sucking brightly coloured sweets and wore unsuitable clothes. I looked at the departure board and saw the destinations: Málaga, Torremolinos, Las Palmas.

As soon as my flight was called I moved, quickly, through the pressing crowd. Soon I was on a half-empty plane bound for the shores of Sicily.

I sat in a row of empty seats and sighed with relief as I looked through the rain-beaded window of the aeroplane, at the fluorescent lights outside, at the damp runway, at the featureless green fields in the distance.

III

The plane pierced the winter-grey clouds and emerged into the open skies. I looked at the horizon in the distance and I experienced a sense of freedom — as if until then my soul had been held captive, buried for centuries inside a tomb of dark, dark slate.

As I looked at the vast blue sky my mind travelled back in time.

Memories of an early Sicilian childhood came flooding into my mind.

My parents took me away from Sicily when I was twelve years old. They migrated to the North of Italy, like many other families in the village.

My father had followed in the footsteps of his brother. His brother had followed in the footsteps of his brother-in-law, and he in turn in the footsteps of his father.

That was the trend then.

They abandoned the land of their fathers to work on the conveyor belts of the new production age.

They wanted to lead modern lives.

They wanted to live in apartment blocks with modern bathrooms, washing machines, telephones, dishwashers. No matter what.

They had already sampled scenes of the New Life on television.

As children we believed that the streets and the cathedrals of the North were built with gold bricks.

That was what we thought then.

I remember the first twenty-four-hour train journey to the North. It took place in November, in the late fifties.

I remember being struck by the beauty of the sea every time the train roared out from the long, dark tunnels.

I remember the empty beaches, the abandoned sea resorts, the lines of closed sun umbrellas on the wet beaches, the raindrops splashing against the window as the train travelled through the dark night, the nests of flickering lights in the jewelled mountains at dusk, the crowded stations, the women selling food and drinks between stations.

I remember one early morning, as the train stopped briefly at a chill mountain station, my father running to the fountain to refill our bottles with fresh water.

My parents had found a flat next to a factory in the outskirts of the city.

I recall the endless noise from the factory engines which made the thin walls of our apartment tremble.

I recall too the metallic smell of the factory chimneys; the smoke-filled sky, the sound of the sirens constantly calling the workers to the conveyor belts.

Each time the sirens sounded streams of workers in blue overalls would go in or out, depending on the time of day.

I remember the deep sadness of not being able to roam in the countryside after school or roll down the sandy slopes and climb the trees as I used to do.

I would look at the misty, grey factories through our window. Look at the high, smoking chimneys. Hear the perpetual sound of the factory engines. Watch the rusty rain falling on the window. Then I would cry, cry and cry.

I became inconsolable. I cried and cried for hours every day. At home and at school they did not know what to do with me.

My eyes became red and tears would spring forth uncontrollably.

I remember the strange rainbow-like colours that appeared on the street in front of our flat every time there was a sudden shower.

I remember the acid, metallic smell of the chimneys which smoked, both day and night.

In the evenings when my parents returned from the factories I would be found lying on my bed. I had lost all my appetite. Lost all the energy I once had. They took me to see a doctor. The doctor told them that I was suffering from loss, from melancholia, from lack of light.

He said to my parents:

"He will adjust. Adjust to the New Life."

He put some cool drops in my red eyes and told them to take me to the country for a week to breathe the mountain air, see the trees, the lakes, the animals.

IV

In Sicily our house stood close to the local church. During religious festivals my mother enjoyed decorating the interior of the baroque church with beautiful flowers and shrubs, many of which she grew herself in a little plot of land behind our house.

Many Sicilians have Arab blood running through their veins.

One can see this in their looks. They are short, with dark olive bodies. They wear mournful expressions on their faces. They can be cunning, corrupt and sensuous. They resemble their North African neighbours.

Our local priest, in contrast, had Norman blood running through his veins.

He had striking Nordic looks. He was tall, well-built, handsome, had fair hair and emerald green eyes.

He was of a kind and simple disposition.

With my father he enjoyed talking about the land, the seasons, the animals and the weather in so far as it affected the crops.

He hardly ever talked to us about his real profession — the Church. Indeed he spent more time on his land than he ever spent preaching or dealing with church affairs.

Behind his back his parishioners often made fun of him; for on many occasions when they were at confession instead of talking to them about religion he asked them about how their husbands had solved this or that particular agricultural problem. He asked whether their husbands' crops had been suffering much from a recent drought, whether they were coping well with the latest irrigation machinery, whether they had bought this or that new tool.

Once he admitted that he often dreamed about various agricultural problems.

As the parishioners told these stories to each other they always had a good laugh.

In the evenings the priest would often come to our house and eat with us the simple meals which my mother prepared. He became part of our family.

He would never come empty-handed to our house.

He brought produce from his land — fruit, olives, wild vegetables, wine, oil and nuts.

Sometimes he arrived carrying in his arms a big bunch of velvety red carnations. The sweet scent would linger in our house for days.

He was always kind to me and would often ask me to sit on his knees while he talked to father. In the church choir I felt that I was in a privileged position in comparison to the other boys.

When he was in our house he would smile at me and affectionately put both his arms around my head. Both my parents were very proud of this close association with our priest who preferred the company of simple people like ourselves to the company of the land-owning classes. For my parents he was an educated and respected figure of authority.

During school holidays he would regularly come to collect me from our house and take me to the country for the day. He had a cart drawn by two strong mules. On these occasions my father would wake me just before dawn. I would then sit next to him on the cart and we would ride together over the stony tracks as the day was beginning to break in the countryside.

One day in May, during harvest time, we went together to the country on one such trip. It was a Sunday and on that day we left the village after he had finished celebrating early morning Mass.

The fields in the countryside were covered in golden wheat ready to be harvested. The roadsides were abundant with wild flowers: yellow poppies, red poppies, purple orchids and corn-marigolds.

For centuries the corn-marigolds had been linked in our village with a religious festival which took place each year in May.

That May morning the air was soft and sweet and the scents of spring were everywhere.

As we rode through the countryside we stopped to gather the sun-yellow corn-marigolds used to make the flower garlands for the festival which our village would celebrate a few days later. That Sunday all the children from the village also went to gather the marigolds from the fields with their friends.

At dusk the children returned to the village with huge bunches of the flowers and the next day the streets, the balconies, terraces and roofs of the houses would be awash with colour. The flowers were separated from their stems and threaded on to long cotton strings. Both ends of the strings were then joined together to form garlands for the festival.

After we had finished gathering the flowers for our garlands, we spent most of the day gathering and tidying the hay.

It was late afternoon when we were preparing to leave the country. The cart had been loaded with hay for the animals in the village. I had placed all the bunches of flowers on top of the hay. While the priest was still in the shed, out of fun and as a surprise for him, I decided to decorate the mules' heads, ears and tails with the flowers.

I climbed, barefooted and wearing only my shorts, on to the cart and sat excitedly on top of the hay waiting for his surprised smile as he came out of the shed.

I waited for a while but he did not emerge from the shed. Then I heard his voice calling me from inside. I came down from the cart and went into the hay-shed.

There I could only see stack upon stack of hay bathed by sunlight filtering through the broken roof tiles. I could not see him.

I realised that he was playing at hide and seek. I shouted: "Where are you hiding? Where are you hiding?". But I received no answer. Then after a while I heard his voice saying that I should look for him in the loft.

I climbed an old and twisted wooden ladder. Once my head was above the ceiling I could only see stacks of hay and more rays of sunlight.

I went into the loft and walked quietly through the hay in the hope of surprising him. Then I saw a crumbling partition wall and went to look behind it. There he was, behind the rustic chalk wall, naked, his body reclining on the loose hay and streaked by the sunlight.

I looked at him, shyly. His green eyes were clear, like the May sky outside. His arms were open, as in an embrace. His face had a gentle, timid expression.

The hair over his body had the colour of the surrounding hay. His erect penis was dewy and quivered, timorously, like spring leaves in the morning breeze. He locked me into his gaze and we stayed like that, in silence, for some time.

Then he stretched his arms towards me and I moved towards him and came to rest over his warm body. His arms closed on me. Then I felt a tightening and a loosening of his embrace.

I saw his face moisten and his eyes meditatively close. We stayed in that embraced position as the blond patterns of sunlight flickered on our bodies.

The following day our village celebrated the arrival of spring with a procession through the narrow, perilous streets. The whole village was awash with the colour of the garlanded flowers. They were round people's necks, on balcony railings, over gates, in the churches. There was colour everywhere.

At midday the heavy dome-shaped shrine, standing on two thick wooden poles, was carried out of the main church by twenty-four men. The men were bare-footed. They wore transparent white tunics on bare bodies and around their waists dangled silken cords.

On their heads they wore black pointed hoods; their eyes gleamed in the morning light. In the centre of the shrine there was a large monstrance containing the consecrated host. The monstrance was made of solid gold and was an image of the radiant sun.

As the procession began to move the brass band began playing cheerful music. In front of the procession there was a line of priests wearing golden robes and scattering incense in the air.

The children were standing on the balconies, on the rooftops, on adults' shoulders and on tree branches from where they threw the garlands of corn-marigold at the moving shrine, screaming with joy.

Then the adults joined in, throwing their garlands and smiling. The shrine and the monstrance were soon covered with hundreds of dazzling yellow garlands. Many of the garlands also landed on the men in the white tunics.

The streets were lined with trees of flowering oleanders and paved with slabs of black lava.

That day I was bursting with excitement. I kept running away from my parents, moving through the crowds, getting close to the brass band, smelling the different trails of incense, waving to my teachers and to school friends. I kept following the shrine as it wound its way through the narrow streets.

The streets were covered in crushed yellow flowers and their spring smell blended pleasingly with the scent of the incense.

The crushed corn-marigolds had made the streets slippery and, as the procession went down a steep street, a couple of the men carrying the shrine slipped on the crushed flowers.

The heavily flowered shrine toppled over and fell on to the chest of one of the men. I was standing close to the shrine and, as it fell on his chest, his warm blood splashed against my face and on to my white shirt.

I remember the fallen man's frozen expression, the shock of seeing his innards mingled with the crushed yellow garlands. His blood was everywhere and his tunic soaked in blood.

I remember the panic, the screams of the women, the brass band changing to playing mournful tunes.

I remember the vibrant sunlight, the vivid colours of that May day, the strong contrasts of light and shade of that distant first Sicilian spring.

As I came out of these distant childhood memories, I noticed a middle-aged man sitting across the aisle of the plane. He had clearly been looking at me while I was engrossed with myself.

He looked at me and smiled. He was intent on starting a conversation. I was struck by the grey, worried expression on his face.

I got up to stretch my legs. On my return I sat closer to his seat and we started talking.

He was, I learned, a London journalist. A disgruntled journalist. Tired of media life. He told me he was leaving London. He had wanted to get away for some time. He was exhausted by the constant "meetings", the traffic jams, the dirt, the pale, corpse-like faces of the people, the desolation of a dying city. He wanted time for himself, time to think. He was tired of being asked to summarize the world's problems in a few hundred words.

He had decided to go. Go.

He was going to Sicily to see the wild flowers of the first spring. Then he was going to take the overnight boat and sail to North Africa. He planned to go to Tangier then perhaps to the Sahara. Then he did not know.

I realised that he had wanted to talk to someone for some time. He talked anxiously and impulsively. The fact that I was a stranger made it easier for him to talk. Later we heard the pilot announce that we were about to approach the shores of Sicily. I returned to my seat and looked outside the window.

In the distance I saw purple mountains enveloped by the heat haze. There were thin filaments of silky white clouds and, below, a fresh and white-blue sea, all shimmering under the sun's light.

The plane landed at 1.30 p.m. and as the doors were opened a flood of salty heat came into the plane. From the plane's steps I saw the first dusty palm tree.

The place looked dead. Desolation all around.

There was not a soul to be seen. The shops were all firmly shut. Outside the terminal there was a tired-looking bus waiting to take the passengers to the city centre.

I had a room booked at the Hotel Barocco.

V

The city streets were deserted and a general air of fatigue was felt everywhere one looked. As we were travelling on the bus I saw row upon row of unfinished buildings. Skeletal constructions.

Close to the city centre I saw luxuriant gardens with many types of palm trees and shrubs with radiant flowers.

I saw an old villa whose long terrazza was covered by a glowing orange bougainvillea. Next to it there was an abandoned palazzo, a shabby palm tree by its main entrance. A dog lay stretched out on the shadow cast by the palm tree .

The outside of the Hotel Barocco had a dark, smoky air. Like the surrounding buildings it had an air of tiredness. Time had taken its toll.

The hotel lobby had a turn-of-the-century charm. At the entrance there was a dignified Sicilian gentleman with a grave expression on his face. He was flanked by two suitcases as he waited for a taxi.

The walls of the lobby were of faded apricot.

A huge mirror, stained by time, reflected the stillness of the place: the subdued blue marble floors: the red-carpeted streaming staircase: a large, dark painting of a nude boy with sensual red lips.

The unsmiling, grey-haired man at reception handed me my room key and said, in a weary tone:

"Sir... life will return to the city later, at about 4.30pm. This is the time when our street market re-opens."

It was 2.30pm and I climbed the marble staircase.

Inside the austere room the long venetian shutters were closed and there was a general air of repose — as if time had stood still for centuries.

Driving from the airport into the city I had noticed that all the windows of the flats and houses were closed as if the inhabitants feared that the brilliant light of Sicily might seep into their rooms.

I opened the shutters and looked into the hotel courtyard. I noticed about a dozen white doves perched over the mossy columns.

I took a shower. I lay on the bed and, as I looked at the columns of the courtyard, I fell into a restful sleep.

I was wakened at 4:30pm by the bustling noise of the city. I dressed quickly and went straight out of the Hotel Barocco.

The receptionist had, of course, been right. The city was transformed. As if for several hours it had been under a spell.

The streets and the squares were crowded with people. The traffic was noisy and dense. Motor scooters appeared from every corner. The shops were all open and the orange buses were bursting with people.

The air was warm and the rugged mountains looking over the city were lit by the colours of an impending sunset.

I decided to walk towards the city's main market which meandered through the city's old baroque streets like a huge serpent.

I entered the market through a side-street lined with stalls selling a variety of ready-to-eat olives. There were heaps of garlicked, pickled, aromatic and spiced olives.

One whole stand was full of olives mixed with wild capers grained with sea salt. Another had green and black olives mixed with pickled carrots. There were stalls selling lush red, white and green North African olives mixed with brightly coloured spices.

As the late afternoon was beginning to turn into dusk the market became increasingly crowded. An overwhelming sensuousness now permeated the whole place.

The olive street opened into a dilapidated baroque square with a small fountain at its centre: this was the almond square. The stalls sold almonds of all types and made in dozens of different ways. There were raw and roasted almonds, almonds in their shells, almond cakes, baby almonds, almond paste, almond sweets, almonds joined by melted raw sugar and made into hard blocks.

Near the fountain there was a group of Murillo boys. They were bare-footed and were playing in the running water.

These are Sicily's Arab boys. They live on the streets, bare-chested. Their smiles often betray a hardened innocence. An innocence tainted by the daily struggle to survive.

The once beautiful baroque buildings around the square were now inhabited by the poor. On one of the decrepit balconies supported by a row of lion's heads there sat a dark-skinned man. He sang popular laments while accompanying himself with the mournful notes of his guitar.

The women on the other balconies were hanging out long lines of washing and singing Sicilian songs of betrayal and love.

After the almond square I reached a long street full of fish stalls. I saw gigantic tuna and swordfishes. There were stalls that sold a rainbow of shellfish. Inside a dark café I saw a group of working men standing near the counter eating oysters and drinking carafes of wine. A man sitting alone at one of the tables was dipping dark bread in a glass of red wine.

Happiness was in the air.

At times I felt as if time had stood still. I had a sense of reassurance, of continuity. I thought that these scenes, these smells, these noises, these colours, these dark cafés had been like that for ever. They had an ancient air. I could have been walking in a market in ancient Egypt, Greece or Rome. There was timelessness here — and everywhere.

The sun began to set behind the purple mountains and the first street lights were switched on. I thought that my senses had had enough for one day.

I climbed the crumbling stairs which led to a terraced restaurant called "Ristorante Shanghai" and sat down for a meal as I looked at the ever-swelling crowd below.

Next morning I woke up early. As I lingered in bed in the darkened room, images from the previous day kept appearing inside my mind. I was looking forward to another day.

I was the first guest to arrive in the breakfast room. They started serving breakfast at seven. A youth in a crisply ironed white jacket came to take the orders. I asked for hot milk, coffee and some fruit. Then I returned to my room for a few moments and was out into the streets by seven-thirty. The city's main Corso was already bustling with traffic and pedestrians.

Before returning to the market I decided to make a detour and went to look at the exterior of the cathedral.

There was the purest blue sky. The buildings were gold with the morning light. When I arrived in front of the cathedral, I sat on its perimeter wall and my eyes were captivated by the warm colour of the stones, the patterns on the walls and the oriental beauty of the whole place. At that hour the square was empty of tourists.

Then suddenly, like an apparition, I saw a procession of young girls in white wedding dresses, with beaded veils over their faces.

They walked slowly, as in a dream, in a single line, beside the cathedral's walls. In their white-gloved hands each held an orange lily. Slowly all the cathedral walls were being encircled by the girls in white dresses.

As the first girl entered the large porticoed entrance, the rich, velvet sound of the organ poured out of the cathedral and incense filled the air.

For a few moments I felt as if I were in a trance. I dared not move, for I feared I might break the morning spell.

Later I returned towards the market to continue my journey. I resumed my exploration of the market at the point where I had interrupted it the previous day.

The next stretch of the market was devoted to aromatic herbs and spices. On the stalls there were heaps of different kinds of oregano, thyme, coriander, lavender, basil, rosemary, and mountains of exotically coloured spices.

I went on and found a small square devoted to many varieties of fruit, then another square devoted to wild vegetables. A whole street was given over to oranges and lemons. I saw large and small, bitter and sweet oranges. Samples of blood oranges and lemons were cut in half to tempt the shoppers with their succulence. The stalls of citrus fruit were decorated with the luxuriant branches of the trees still bearing their blossom.

After a while I walked into a wide crowded street lined with stalls selling meat. Here were row upon row of carcasses of skinned animals hanging along the street. Certain stalls specialized in selling only lambs, others beef, others offal.

There were tongues, brains, kidneys, eyes and hearts on sale.

The vendors, whose white overalls and faces were splattered with bloodstains, held up chunks of raw meat to the passing crowd, praising its freshness and its quality.

All around me was an orgy of slaughter and blood. I began to feel anxious and started walking faster towards the next section of the market — when I suddenly heard the sound of gunshots. For a moment I thought that the shots came from a nearby slaughterhouse. But the sound was too close and reverberated strongly inside my ears.

Then I saw people screaming and running in all directions. I saw two men with pointed black hoods screech out of the panic-stricken crowd on a motor-bike. They waved their guns at the people in order to make a fast escape.

As the gunmen vanished through the decaying baroque sidestreets, a crowd gathered round one of the meat stalls. I too followed my crowd instinct and went to look.

There I saw a scene of carnage.

There were huge carcasses of meat on the pavement. Lying over and between the carcasses of meat were the bodies of three young men perforated by gunshot wounds.

Their heads and chests had become springs of blood and their eyes were frozen in astonishment.

The midday sun accentuated the violence of the massacre.

The Carabinieri, in elegant uniforms and holding submachine guns, cordoned off the area while photographers from the local newspapers recorded the gruesome facts with their cameras.

Some journalists attempted to extract some information from the people who had witnessed the killings.

But they all shook their heads.

They had seen nothing.

Heard nothing.

I walked towards the seafront and went to sit at the pier café near the port and, while the big ships moved slowly around me, I felt for the second time in two days the sheer sensuousness of the place, a sensuousness inflamed by the violent sunlight of Sicily.

After finishing my drink, I strolled along the seafront and returned, by taxi, to my austere room at the Hotel Barocco.

I lay on the bed and closed my eyes but the image of the massacre kept appearing vividly inside my mind.

As I lay on my bed, I thought of Caravaggio.

Of the strange yet, richly beautiful depictions of human violence.

Of the erotic power of his human figures.

Of his dramatic use of darkness and light.

Of his hurried escape to Sicily from a charge of murder.

Then ... I slept.

That afternoon I walked for about two hours in the oldest part of the city. I stopped to look at some courtyards which were once part of beautiful palaces and were now in semi-ruin. The courtyards still had an air of enchantment: one could feel and smell the cool stillness of time.

They were half-lit by the spring light. Pots of flowers encircled the central fountains and the jasmine was often seen intertwined with the columns. An occasional palm tree stood in a corner. Some had fragments of statues: a headless torso, an armless female figure, the remains of a youth ...

I entered an empty church all decorated with orange lilies — the lilies of the first communion. I saw an abandoned palazzo whose walls were covered by russet wild-flowering oleander.

I walked into an old square which had at its centre a giant magnolia tree in full blossom. Its lush leaves touched the balconies of the surrounding buildings. Below there was a boxed garden with herbs and a lovely coolness permeated the square. Many of the magnolia's branches had released roots to the ground which then rooted themselves in the earth below.

Near the boxed garden I saw a small, empty café. I decided to rest beneath the shade of the magnolia. It was 4:30pm and the city was beginning to come alive again. A gentle breeze was coming from the nearby sea.

As I looked around the square, I noticed at its other end a cinema. It had a rather dusty and sleepy look. I saw that middle-aged men were drifting into it. They wore elegant dark suits, some had moustaches, and others were in uniforms. They looked like dignified Sicilian gentlemen. They had sombre and serious expressions.

I naturally became curious as to what they were going to watch inside that cinema at that hour of the afternoon. I paid for my iced coffee and walked towards the cinema.

The board outside was covered with a sky-blue sheet of paper with a stapled notice simply saying "Primo Tempo" — meaning that the first half of the film was already showing.

I bought a ticket. Behind the counter there was an unsmiling woman in her fifties. She had dark hair and wore black mourning clothes. In her arms she held a sleeping child. As I asked her for a ticket she looked at me in a cursory way and handed it to me.

I walked towards the screening hall and opened two big padded doors. I came across several layers of thick velvet curtains. As I opened the curtains, I was temporarily blinded by the fierce contrast of the outside light and darkness inside.

I had to stand still for a while until my eyesight adjusted to the darkness. So I firmly closed my eyes for a few seconds and then re-opened them. In the giant screen in front of me I saw the image of a woman copulating with a man while several other naked men masturbated and fondled each other near them.

I then began to feel the presence of men all around me. As my eyes slowly adjusted to the darkness a whole new picture began to unfold around me. I noticed that the men inside the cinema were not interested in the film being shown on the screen.

To my left there was a small group of men kissing and fondling each other. Some men were on their knees. To my right there was an older, distinguished-looking man, in a passionate embrace with a younger man. In the seats I saw men masturbating each other. There was a naked man going up and down the main aisle with an erect penis. Other men were making love on the carpeted red floor. There were also soldiers, sailors and carabinieri in their uniforms. I saw many men, obvious members of the Sicilian establishment, engaged in scenes of orgy, sex and love. Many of the encounters were just sex while others had about them a touching tenderness.

As I stepped into the street outside I was once again blinded by the violence of the light. I stood still for several minutes with my eyes firmly closed, then I reopened my eyes and walked towards the hotel.

VI

The following afternoon I had arranged to have tea with the Sicilian lady whose telephone number I had been given in London. She taught English literature at the University and she was a widow. She lived alone in the old part of the city in a palazzo which had once belonged to her aristocratic ancestors.

An apartment had been carved out from the rest of the decaying structure. To reach this I climbed a windowless, white-marbled staircase. She lived at the top of the building and her apartment overlooked a courtyard with hibiscus trees in red, bell-like flowers.

She was a woman in her mid-fifties, tall, with tidy brown hair. She wore a long evening dress, in twilight blue, with beaded buttercup stones.

Melancholy dripped from her dark, chestnut eyes.

As I came in she briefly smiled while avoiding looking at me straight into my eyes — as if afraid I might read her innermost secrets.

Her day housekeeper brought in a tray with English tea and biscuits.

I was struck by the restlessness of my hostess. She began to pace nervously up and down the richly tapestried drawing room.

She first told me that her husband had been an architect and had restored the apartment. As she walked around the long rectangular room she held in her hands a silver-framed photograph of her husband standing on a beach.

Then she said: "You see, this treasure-chest once belonged to the Arab Emirs. It is inlaid with precious African stones... These are rosewood cabinets. They are inlaid with mother-of-pearl depicting various stages of the peach blossom. They once belonged to the Norman kings."

"Above the sofa," she continued, "is the only surviving fragment of a twelfth-century Byzantine mosaic which represents the figure of Christ. The complete mosaic was on the wall behind the altar of our chapel. It was bombed in the last war."

Then she told me of the death of her husband. How one winter morning, soon after he'd completed the restoration of the apartment, she had found him lying next to her — frozen in death.

She talked of her continual urge to go out, to leave the apartment. She said that she accepted every dinner invitation no matter with whom. She went out to every arts event that took place in the city, no matter how trivial. It was better, she thought, than being alone in her apartment.

She had travelled abroad a great deal. She had spent a long summer in the Highlands of Scotland where she had stayed in a former hunting lodge by a loch. She had spent the early mornings and the dusks walking around the loch.

She had been a month in Tangier where she had passed hours every day just sitting at the Café de Paris drinking mint tea and looking at the passing crowds.

She had also been to San Francisco. There she had dined every evening in the same gay restaurant in the Castro district looking tenderly at all the men in love.

But she had always wanted to go back to Sicily. Once there, though, she was again assailed by the urge to leave. She had found these years exhausting. She could not find peace anywhere.

Then, suddenly, she looked at her watch with her mournful eyes and said: "You'll have to excuse me. I must leave. I'm going to the opera tonight. Please come and visit me before you leave our island."

I did not call her again on that day. I had decided to leave the city and head for the countryside and toward the sea.

VII

Early next morning I went to a car rental centre close to the hotel and left the city behind.

I felt a strong desire to see the countryside in the first spring, feel the fresh air and smell the scent of the sea before the heat took its grip.

I wanted to see the spring flowers and linger among the ruins of ancient temples.

I wanted to walk barefoot along a sandy beach and inhale the salty air.

I wanted to look at the countless stars in the deep, black night, hear the sound of grasshoppers, see the glow-worms shining in the gleaming night sky.

I took the motorway towards the ancient temple of Segesta. Within fifteen minutes the bustle and noises of the city were behind me.

As I drove along the empty motorway, flanked on one side by the mountains, the blue, shining sea often appeared and then vanished.

The motorway was lined on both sides with globed oleander trees in flower. There were long stretches where the flowers would be white on both sides, then stretches where they would be all pink, then ruby red, then orange.

The centre of the motorway was lined with flowering almond trees. Clouds of the pink-white petals often landed on the windscreen.

After about an hour of driving along the motorway, I saw a sign showing the way to the temples.

The small road meandered through hillsides and meadows adorned with wild spring flowers.

Later I stopped at a side lane overlooking a little valley which was covered with shrubby palm trees.

Nearby there was the view of a burned-out orchard overgrown with blooming thistles.

I took a walk through a field carpeted by red poppies. Then I went through a field of flowering mints and oregano. I walked up a slope covered with Sicilian wild roses, roses whose petals flew at the slightest breeze.

I reached the top of a hill.

From there I saw a scene of pure enchantment.

A small, neatly-kept, orchard of lemon trees whose yellow fruits weighed down the leafy branches.

The wooden perimeter fence was covered by climbing red roses.

The ground was full of purple orchids.

A lonely farmer wearing black clothes and a black cap was digging in a corner.

The faint sound of water could be heard breaking through rocks.

On a ridge in the distance there was a row of old eucalyptus trees whose silver-green leaves swayed in the wind.

Beyond, perched on a hilltop, there were the cool stones of an ancient temple bathed in the gold morning light.

I stood there,
    motionless,
        unable to move,
            unthinking,
unnoticed,
    while,
        the warm spring breeze blew on my face.
            Then, I wept,
                quietly —
                    and with happiness.

*

Summer Light

I

He had just returned from his early morning walk. It was in May 1899.

On that cool morning the luminous sea mist was still hovering over the seashores of northern Norway.

The dark winter months had come to a temporary close and the whole landscape was now flooded by the brilliant summer light of Scandinavia.

The gleaming black waters of the sea had calmed and the cold waves lapped against the cliffs below his house.

Storms of black-backed seagulls rejoiced in the invigorating freshness of the early summer.

They glided,

they dived,

they climbed,

they dropped, like pebbles, towards the sea.

Then, they climbed, again, up towards the misty sky, to be carried away by a passing air current.

They reigned, undisturbed, over the seashore and their sharp sounds reverberated throughout the fjord countryside. Their cries were faintly heard by the inhabitants of the nearest village, set in the midst of blossoming apple orchards at the end of the fjord.

Inside a deep sea-gorge three silent seagulls hung motionless, suspended in mid-air, the mist around their bodies, oblivious to the clatter generated by their neighbours. Occasionally they flapped their wings, as if trying to liberate their bodies from the enveloping mist.

Streams of different strengths released their limpid waters through the rugged slate walls of the sea-gorge down and into the sea.

Later that morning, as the Nordic light gathered intensity, it would burn off the mist over the seashore, revealing the airy and melancholic beauty of the coastline, the treeless moorlands with touches of browns, purples and yellow, the primeval shrubs bent by the unceasing cold winds of the long winter months, the greenest of valleys and meadows, the clearest of mountain waters, the most fleeting, dream-like of wild spring flowers...

The snow-covered mountains in the distance told of the continued presence of winter, lurking like a dark shadow, behind this temporary release of light and joy.

On the moorlands the pungent gorses displayed their yellow pearl-shaped flowers while the tender primroses hid shyly beneath the winter-worn shrubs.

Timorous young birds often burst out of the undergrowth on their first summer flight.

II

His house stood at the end of a long narrow fjord. He had had it built of solid cliff stone, so that it would be capable of withstanding the fiercest winter storm.

Seen from a distance it was part of the landscape. During the early morning mists it appeared to vanish, as if washed away by the sea waves.

The heart of the house was a long rectangular room. Its three large windows looked towards the sea. It had a dark slate floor and an open fireplace with logs heaped on the left hand side. The room was sparsely furnished. There was a large brown desk in front of the middle window, a couple of chairs and, close to the fireplace, a comfortable winged chair with a footstool. The walls were white and bare.

On the left of his desk, leaning against a group of finely bound books of German poetry and aphorisms, was a small painting in an intricate, golden frame.

It depicted a winter landscape with snow, glowing in the early evening light, a figure with crutches sitting on the trunk of a fallen oak tree, fresh shoots of green grass piercing through new winter snow, a frozen pond with a group of young and bare birch trees on one of its banks, the ruins of an ancient abbey. A tall wooden cross rose from its Gothic ruins and, piercing the dusky, golden sky, a desiccated figure of Christ hanging from the cross, a rusty iron crown on his head.

The painting had been presented to him at a civic reception in Berlin two months earlier at the end of a series of concerts to celebrate his fiftieth birthday. He was a composer.

He had found the whole evening a strain, for he was by nature a shy, reserved man, who found formal occasions awkward, even embarrassing. Soon after the evening began his mind switched off. He heard nothing but a murmur of distant voices as he drifted off on the sea of his own consciousness. He looked with absent eyes at the glittering crowds. He smiled sometimes, with his gentle, drooping eyes.

The concerts had been conceived by a great admirer of his music, the leading German conductor of the period, who was famous throughout Germany as much for his eccentric, stormy personality as for his musical genius.

His concerts were governed by the states of his violently changing moods. If during a concert his mood changed and darkened he would treat both orchestra and audience with disdain, even with contempt.

While he was passionately conducting one of the composer's most engaging Nordic symphonies, and while the whole audience was in a state of rapturous delight, he angrily ordered the players to stop and, turning to his astonished audience, he began to shout abuse at the German nation for neglecting one of its greatest thinkers whose unique work contained, for him, the distilled soul of the German people.

As he expressed these thoughts, sweat came pouring down his face, dripping down towards his starched collar and wetting his brilliantly white shirt. The entire audience, including the composer who was flanked by city dignitaries, soon came out of their perplexed state and looked at him with clear, affectionate understanding. Once he had finished his speech, he turned, calmly, to the orchestra and resumed the concert with added ardour and fearless passion.

III

Since he had been appointed Professor of Composition at the University of Copenhagen ten years earlier the composer had led a longed-for tranquil existence. The long years of wandering through the musical circles of Berlin, Leipzig and Vienna had finally ended. And towards the end of his thirties he seemed to have been seized by an overwhelming sense of weariness.

What had once invigorated and stimulated his mind had come to infinitely tire and unsettle him. For some years he had been longing to lead a solitary life, a life of work inspired by the natural beauty of his native country.

For over a decade now he had tutored in Copenhagen, returning regularly, for several months at a time, to his house by the fjord.

While in Copenhagen he tended to shy away from the social life of the university. But he enjoyed the presence of his students. He found their enthusiasm for music rewarding, and particularly enjoyed his weekly seminars, when he would be surrounded by them. He did not like to talk about his own music and discouraged the students from asking him too many questions. He spoke to them in a low, warm voice. Occasionally he would smile as his eyes looked down at the wooden table littered with empty coffee-stained cups.

In the afternoons he often went for walks along the city's canals. Sometimes he would stop at a café by the water's edge for a hot drink.

Once inside the café he freed himself of his old army coat, bought at the time of his student days in Leipzig. He sat by the window, wiped the steamed glass, and then gazed contentedly at the passing crowds, at the elegant women in their dark overcoats with fur collars round their long necks, at the occasional group of noisy students, at the black horse-drawn carriages taking people to the steam boats, at the footsteps engraved in the fresh winter snow...

IV

That early May morning, as he returned from his walk, the postman was waiting for him. He had cycled from the nearest village at the end of the fjord. He was a jovial man in his early sixties, with a white beard, grey fuzzy hair, burning red cheeks and smiling green eyes.

He handed a batch of letters to the composer and made a few witty remarks, which he himself enjoyed a great deal. Then he began whistling and mounted his solid, black-framed bicycle and rode along the fjord path, occasionally tilting to one side as the seagulls clattered over and past his head.

With the letters under his left arm, the composer opened the front door of his house. The long corridor was illuminated by the light seeping through the half-closed door of his study.

He looked towards the study. By his desk, he saw the back of a tall and slim female figure, in a long, black dress, her long hair gathered in a neat knot behind her neck.

He paused and remained silent, so as not to disturb her at her work. He observed her composed movements. She first moved his papers from the desk. Placed them on the chair and polished the desk. She then returned his papers to the same place. With both hands resting on his desk, she looked at the luminous mist outside as the seagulls came noisily and carelessly past the window.

He saw her move away from the desk, then return a few moments later with a large vase of clear glass. It had a tubular shape and overflowed with old garden roses, foxgloves and branches of flowering honeysuckle.

As he observed this the waves below his house could be faintly heard.

Where he stood in the corridor there was a plain, white chair which almost touched the wall. He had involuntarily touched it several times, enjoying its wooden texture with his hand.

He placed the letters on the white chair, removed his coat, then his walking boots. He collected the letters and walked towards his study.

As he opened the door the strong morning light, like a large sea wave, came flooding into the corridor. He entered the room and saw the woman kneeling in front of the fireplace, lighting the logs.

As she felt his presence inside the room, still on her knees, she turned round, looked at the composer and smiled, shyly. She got up and left the room, gently closing the door behind her.

V

He placed the letters on his desk and sat down. Then he looked outside the window. The mist had suddenly vanished, revealing the dazzling beauty of sea, the sunlit green banks of the fjord, the serenity of a luminous landscape.

He opened the window, took several deep breaths of cool air and felt an invigorating sense of freshness penetrate his being. He felt calmly happy, the kind of happiness which would sustain him during the months he was going to spend there, in his house by the fjord.

He opened his letters one by one. The business letters from the university or from his Leipzig publisher he placed unread inside the drawer.

His attention was drawn by a brown envelope which bore the postmark "Charlottenburg, Berlin". He became curious as to who the sender might be. Before opening the earth-brown envelope he inspected the handwriting. Then he felt the texture of the paper with his fingers. It became obvious to him that it did not contain an official letter from the City of Berlin nor did it contain a letter from the eccentric German conductor who had invited him there last month.

He decided to open the letter and inserted his old pine-wood penknife along its edge. He unfolded it. His eyes went straight to the first paragraph.

*P*lease *forgive my intrusion into your life and for disturbing you in your work. But I felt I must write to you to explain some of the extraordinary effects that your music has had within my soul.*

As I was listening to the performances of your music in Berlin last month I relived a sweet and tragic episode of my childhood. As I listened to the music, a powerful and turbulent current overcame my being. I felt anguished and I wept.

For several days afterwards, I pleaded with your publishers in Leipzig to give me your summer address so that I could write to you.

I am a young man, a painter, a Berliner in my last year at the Art Institute.

My father was a timber merchant who frequently travelled to Scandinavia on business. He was serious and hardworking and had founded a small company which specialised in importing pinewood into Germany. He was a good and kind father and for some time he had promised to take me on one of his trips to Scandinavia. For he knew what a deep impression Nature made on me. He finally kept his promise and when I was twelve years old we travelled together to Norway. It was in the spring.

I was full of excitement. It was my first long train journey, one which has made a deep impression on my life.

During all the time we were travelling I kept my eyes fixed on the window. I was enchanted by all the beautiful scenes which Nature offered me. The train's swift motion added an extra dimension of beauty to the scenes which flitted past.

The roaring of the train's engines, the metallic sound of the wheels rolling over the rails, the huge puffs of dark steam coming out of the train as we crossed the flat landscape of northern Germany, the hooting as the train approached a blind bend — all this gave infinite pleasure to my young, impressionable heart.

After my father had finished his business in Oslo he took me for a two-week tour of northern Norway. He knew that I longed to breathe the crisp fjord air and to see dark, deep waters, seabirds, the light of a Nordic night, the blazing colours of the midnight sun...

As I was listening to your music I remembered the primroses, the birch woods, the forgotten moorlands, the countless streams, the primeval dawns, the waters which poured out of the earth, the blue glaciers, the ancient foxgloves growing in the hedgerows and the fresh, invigorating air of a Scandinavian spring.

During our trip we stayed at magnificent country hotels set in green valleys. There were strangely dark, still lakes, flowering fruit orchards whose petals resembled tinted snowflakes...

One evening, after we had finished our dinner, we went for a walk around the lake. Then we returned to our hotel room to watch the midnight sun from our bed.

We had completely opened the curtains. Our bed faced the double window and we had panoramic views over the lake and the open sky.

As the sun was coming to rest on the horizon, the sky became streaked with shades of red, yellow, purple and pearly white. We were both enchanted by this wonderful spectacle of nature.

My father and I were lying next to each other on the bed, our shoulders resting on the soft pillows. My head was on his chest and, in the stillness of the night, I could hear the beats of his heart as the warm currents of his breath caressed my face.

All this had a soothing effect and, with my father's arms around my body, I fell into a restful sleep.

But after about an hour we were woken by a sudden explosion. We heard some faint screams. We saw the curtains in our room on fire. Immediately after, the wooden frames began smoking, releasing a fragrance of pine. Then we heard the noise of cracking glass. The night breeze began blowing the burning curtains towards the midnight sun. The lake in front of the hotel which reflected the lighted sky of the midnight sun seemed also to have caught fire.

My father took me up into his arms. We rushed out of the room, down the spacious wooden staircases and towards the lawn outside. We heard the hotel staff shouting "Fire! Fire! Out! Out!". We heard children screaming and saw men and women still in their nightclothes, tumbling down the stairs. The hotel staff assembled us in a group at the end of the lawn, close to an herbaceous border full of rosemary, sage, thyme and honeysuckle over the thick brick wall.

We stood silent, close to each other, warmed by the scented air, as we watched the flames engulf the hotel against the background of a blazing sky.

As I was listening to your music, all these memories returned, burning inside my mind. I experienced waves of emotion. Happiness, despair, loss and a feeling of strange emptiness. After our return to Berlin we were strolling together one Sunday morning in the Tiergarten when my dear father had a sudden heart attack. He clutched my hand hard. I saw his eyes bulge. Then he fell on the wet grass. I cried for help. But he died, there, in front of my very eyes. I saw the expression in his face freeze, become like the wooden heads he sometimes sculpted during his spare time.

As I listened to your music, I relived the memory of my father holding me in his arms, of the hotel in roaring flames, the streaked, red sky, the walks through the birch woods, the rapids flowing through the pine-scented mountains, the red salmon flying upstream towards the blue glaciers, the snowdrops, white as the snow which encircled the mountain peaks...

There were moments in your Fifth Symphony when I remembered walking along the edge of a fjord in the early morning mist, moments when I recalled wandering over a purple-heathered moor, moments when I saw the bare, empty, silent rooms of our hotel by that strange still lake, whose water was illuminated by the Nordic light. There were moments when I saw a spring at its source which gathered strength as it ran its course, moments when I remembered groups of grazing reindeer on a cold, bare, treeless mountainside carpeted with fresh snow...

Like Nature, your music, transcends human life. It stands alone, like an ancient tree on a forgotten moor. It has no purpose.

It conveys no message of human improvement, no hope, no promise, no freedom. It is constituted of pure expressive force. It is energy, unfettered energy.

Like a mountain stream it springs,
it runs and
it ends in Nature, in itself.

Your music has rekindled my desire to visit the land of my sweetest holiday. I would like your permission to visit you in order to paint a portrait of you at midnight, as the sun approaches the horizon. To paint your eyes reflecting the colours of the Nordic dusk. To see again the sky set on fire.

I trust you will grant me this request and will allow me to come before spring fades into autumn and winter.

The composer read the letter slowly, often pausing. While reading it, he had fleeting sensations that his blood was burning.

He savoured every sentence, every word.

He was moved.

Touched by the young man's enthusiasm, by his
response to both nature and his own music.

He knew he could not refuse the request.

His answer was, like all his responses, extremely brief:

*I welcome a visit from you on condition that we do not
talk about my music.*

You see, I value silence.

*I grant your request to paint my portrait by the mid-
night sun.*

On a separate sheet of paper he wrote instructions
about how to reach the house.

VI

Three weeks later the young painter arrived at his
house. June was coming to an end and the Nordic
summer light had reached its peak.

For three months a silence based on a common
understanding pervaded their companionship.

A warmth of feeling was also immediately established
between the two.

They spent many hours together in the same room;
occasionally they would glance at each other, but each
was engaged in his own work.

A regular pattern of life was established. At daybreak
they would go out for a two-hour walk. Each day they
tried different routes.

Some days they would walk along the coastal path even
when it was shrouded in mist, other days they would take
the path through the pine woods, at yet other times they
would walk along the fjord banks and through the
flowering fruit orchards whose rosy blossoms were now
replaced by green leaves.

After their walks they returned to the house to settle down to work. The young painter would often go out again to draw or paint in a meadow or by the seashore. At around one o'clock they would meet again and sit down to a light lunch of fruit and vegetables. Occasionally, at low tide, they would go to one of their favourite enclosed bays. They would walk on the exposed sand and then gather mussels on the black, wet rocks.

They would also go for day-long mountain rambles and enjoy strolling over the crisp snow.

At midnight, as the sun settled to rest on the horizon, the composer would sit for an hour by the large open window and, as he looked towards the setting sun, the young painter would continue his portrait.

The weeks passed, and the mountain snow, like lava from an active volcano, was descending slowly to cover the green valleys. The tops of the pine trees were now frosted.

Bright sunlight was now being replaced by moonlight, which dominated both day and night. The sea began to be restless.

One morning towards the end of September as they were walking through a pine wood, the composer broke his silence. They sat down on a fallen tree trunk; around them clumps of pastel crocuses were piercing the snow and the moist dead leaves. Above them the moon released a fresh, cooling light over the entire landscape.

The composer looked at the young man with his drooping, gentle eyes and said:

"I long to see the land where the lemon and orange trees grow.

I long to stand on ancient soil.

I long to see the fallen stones of a temple under a clear blue sky.

I long to climb the steps of an ancient theatre and to see a snow-capped volcano in the distance.

I long to walk through an olive orchard fanned by the early morning breeze.

I long to see sun-darkened bodies."

A few days later they left the house by the fjord, and rode together through a moonlit landscape, leaving the winter-berried slopes of northern Norway, travelling onward, towards the land of the flowering almond, towards the land sweetly scented by the orange blossoms.

*

An Orderly Existence

I

Luis Federico Alba is in his mid-forties and the father of a young and beautiful daughter.

He lives in a spacious, elegant apartment block in the centre of Madrid.

He is a rather handsome man, the way professional Mediterranean men can be.

Dark and wavy brown hair, medium height, neither slim nor fat. His gleaming brown eyes are alert and with a tinge of sadness.

His aesthetic vision can be expressed in these two words: understated classicism.

This vision is reflected in the way he has chosen to furnish (indeed some would say positively underfurnish) his apartment on the sixth floor.

He has left most of his white walls uncluttered, with only the occasional seventeenth or eighteenth century Spanish architectural drawing.

In a strategically visual position he has placed the only painting in his possession, of which he is extremely fond.

The painting depicts a desolate and timeless figure standing with his shadow at the corner of an equally timeless Italian porticoed square.

II

When he returned home from his office, especially during the unbearably hot summer months, and when his daughter was still in good health and away at university, he would quickly undress and take a shower, alternating its flow from hot to cold.

Then, he would lie naked for a while on his bed, looking at the sunset and just thinking. This was usually his favourite time of the evening.

As he dried his brown, smooth and muscular body he would often conceive some of his best ideas concerning work or other personal matters.

Although he had been affectionately attached to his wife, since her death from an air accident five years earlier, he had, deep down, really enjoyed his regained freedom.

While his daughter was at a private boarding school and then at university, he had happily spent his evenings reading classic literature.

Sometimes he would go to a piano or cello recital — these two instruments, especially when unaccompanied, being his favourites; for, in his view, as solo instruments they were capable of expressing a higher form of musical individuality than when they were submerged by the full weight of a large orchestra.

II

His life had, in other words, an orderly existence. It resembled the cool regularity of the porticoed square of his much-loved painting hanging in his drawing room.

But now the regularity of his life has been disrupted once again.

For some months his beloved daughter has been seriously ill. She is now lying, pale and sad, in the brilliantly white room of a large hospital.

The only colours in the room are to be found in the vase full of red roses which her father brings to her almost daily.

The father is distressed to see his daughter helplessly wasting away before his own eyes. His brown eyes express a subtle, Lorcaian anguish — as if life itself was for him a source of distress.

He is now sitting on the edge of his daughter's bed tenderly looking at her pale face and gently holding her hand.

The only slight noise to be heard is the humming of the passing traffic outside the building. Occasionally she gives her father a glance, fully conscious of her imminent fate.

After a while the doors open to reveal a strikingly tall female figure, all in white. She whispers to the father that the doctors want to see him.

He releases his daughter's hand and leaves the room. At the other end of the long shining corridor, in a spacious light room, two doctors await him.

He listens with anticipation to what they have to say. They inform him that his daughter has now only days, perhaps hours, to live. They suggest that she should spend the time which she has left in familiar surroundings, her own home.

III

While preparations are being made for his daughter's transfer to his apartment he is seized by a reflective mood.

And while a group of nurses make the preparations for wheeling his daughter to a waiting ambulance, he wonders how he could give her a last glimpse of happiness.

He remembers a childhood friend of hers with whom she had often played. He was now a young man studying medicine at the city's main university.

Like her, he was shy, generous and handsome in a rather inconspicuous way. He acts upon his thought and asks the nurses to wait while he makes a telephone call.

The young man, naturally distressed to learn of the state of his childhood friend, agrees immediately to join them at the father's apartment. They then continue the brief journey to the waiting ambulance.

Once inside the father whispers the news about the friend to his daughter.

She responds with a faint smile.

IV

When they arrive in front of the apartment block the nurses wheel his daughter to the lift.

In front of the door he thanks the nurses for all their help and then insists on making the final preparations for his daughter's arrival at home.

He then opens his flat's door and wheels his daughter through the long marbled entrance hall and the large drawing room towards her bedroom.

But on reaching the double windows of the drawing room he suddenly stops and opens the windows wide, as if to take a breath of fresh air.

Then, calmly, he lifts his daughter from the bed. With her body stretched on both his arms he gazes at the flaming orange sunset.

He brings her to the edge of the windows and releases his daughter's body into the emptiness of the street below.

A few seconds later her body lies in a pool of blood. The scene is witnessed in disbelief and horror by the young man who had just arrived and the nurses on their way out of the apartment block.

The young man rushes to where her body lies and touches her. On touching her body, her head and shoulder slowly lift towards him as she releases a heartbreaking scream before collapsing once again.

*

Frosted Eyes

I

It was in late October, 4.30 p.m., in the City of London, on a drizzling, cold evening when John Yeadon had just finished his day's work at the bank.

The amber of the city lights, the heaviness of the traffic fumes, and the misty greyness of a wet, early winter's night gave the sky a rusty, metallic colour.

He'd been waiting in a queue at the bus stop for about five minutes. There were six people in front of him and a few others had joined the queue almost immediately after he'd arrived. They were all holding umbrellas in their hands. Their faces were pale and drawn and none of them had engaged in conversation. They were oblivious of those around them.

Masses of people, looking frightened like rats, were running out of every building. They opened umbrellas, crossed streets, went down passageways, waved at passing taxis and picked up the evening paper at street corners. Thousands rushed to the railway stations or went down iron stairs to catch underground trains.

Amid the slow-moving traffic, delivery motorbikes, ridden by fearsome men, tore through the narrow spaces between cars, taxis and buses.

Sometimes they could be seen driving fast through traffic lights which were about to turn red. At other times they stopped, suddenly — and grudgingly — at a pedestrian crossing, and then vanished again into the murky, rainy night.

John Yeadon was wearing a beige raincoat and a brown tweed cap. He held black leather gloves in his hands and had the bank's briefcase wedged between his legs on the wet pavement.

He was waiting for the No. 86 bus.

The bus would take him through Fleet Street, the Strand and Trafalgar Square to his destination — Piccadilly Circus. From there he would stroll through the busy, crowded streets of the West End to his favourite café in Soho.

Unlike his colleagues at the Bank who, soon after work, returned in crowds to their homes in the suburbs, he was filled with dismay at the thought of going straight home.

He'd been going to the same café for well over twenty years. Not that he could in any way be thought a bohemian type. He was, in fact, a most ordinary man. A man with a regular job. A man who wore pin-striped polyester suits bought in the sales at Marks & Spencer, Oxford Street.

He was a man content with the way his career at the bank had developed.

He had started at the bank as a simple clerk and was then promoted to cashier. After several years and a lot of hard work, he was made an Assistant to the Deputy Chief Cashier. When the Chief Cashier came to retire, he became Deputy to the Chief Cashier.

Finally, after fifteen years of working at the same City branch and at the age of only thirty-five, John Yeadon was promoted, when his boss was transferred to a branch nearer to his home in Surrey, to the job of Chief Cashier.

Under his direct personal responsibility, he had a Deputy Chief Cashier, several assistants to the Deputy Chief Cashier and a small army of junior cashiers who had joined the bank after obtaining four 'O' Levels, one of which, of course, had to be in Maths.

When he telephoned his widowed mother to tell her the news, she was, naturally, very proud of her son who had become Chief Cashier at a national bank.

Within a few hours the news of his promotion had spread throughout the whole of his home town in Yorkshire.

John Yeadon was now in his middle-forties and had been Chief Cashier at the bank for over ten years. He was a clean-shaven, quietly-spoken and discreetly good-looking man.

His dark hair was brushed backwards to reveal a shy and vulnerable face.

His shyness was made the more apparent by the fact that, unlike most of his colleagues, he didn't wear spectacles.

When he talked to his staff, he avoided looking straight into their eyes — as if afraid they might read into his. His brownish eyes had a touch of haziness about them — as if he were trying to see ahead through a veil of morning mist.

At work his good-natured character was not always to his advantage, for, whenever changes had to be made in the way the staff worked, he was afraid to upset them. Of course, they resisted any changes, which would, in their view, adversely affect them. Indeed on some occasions he had to seek the Manager's intervention in order to get through their obstinate unwillingness to absorb any change.

If he had to make any of his staff redundant, as had indeed once happened during a recent recession in the banking industry, he went, poor man, into a panic and had nightmares about it.

Whom would he choose?

How would he tell them?

How would they react to the news?

What would happen to their houses in Redhill, Virginia Water, Lewisham...?

Then he would think of the repercussions of unemployment on their families. Losing their jobs meant losing the benefits associated with working with a big bank, such as the generous mortgage facilities.

It was an agony for him to decide when the moment came.

And yet he knew he had to do it.

It was required of him.

It was part of his job, at times, to have to ruin other people's lives.

And he did it.

After he'd told them the news he couldn't bear to see their faces. He found painful their silence at the office as they counted the days, weeks, months and even hours which remained to them at the bank.

II

John Yeadon had first come up to London from his native Yorkshire when he was a young lad. He'd come to do a one-year course in accountancy.

It was during this first year in London that he discovered his favourite café in the heart of Soho, situated in a small side street, just off Dean Street.

It happened one autumn evening soon after the start of his course. He was walking aimlessly through the crowded streets of Soho when he had his first glimpse of the café.

He was first struck by its window which displayed a tall wedding cake. At the top of the cake there were two plastic figurines of a bride and groom in a gaily dancing pose.

Behind the steamed glass of the window there was a long, white beaded veil and on both sides of the cake there were several other smaller cakes — Saint Honorés, Black Forest Gateaux, Strawberry and Blackberry Flans...

The base of the window, which was decorated with a glittering Christmas-like paper, was covered with pink and white confetti.

To the right of the café there was a porn shop which displayed erotic magazines and women's fancy underwear.

To the left there was an open door and a flight of steep, sleazy stairs. On the door there were bells with names such as Matilda, Plume, Françoise, Brigitte.

As he was looking at the window, he'd noticed men in business suits going up those steep stairs.

That first evening he had lingered for a while looking at the steamed window of the café and gazed through the beaded veil, at the people crowded together along the tables and the waitresses busily serving the customers.

He became fascinated by the atmosphere of the café. He decided not to go in for he feared it might be too expensive. So he promised himself that he would return another time, after the first instalment of his grant had been paid into his bank account.

As he was about to leave, he looked again at the cakes and was assailed by doubt.

Was the huge wedding cake in the centre real or fake? He couldn't decide.

III

During his first year in London, he rented a poorly furnished room in one of the streets opposite King's Cross Station, above a take-away kebab shop.

The place had the advantage of being close both to his college in Russell Square and to Euston Station from which he could catch the train to see his mother in Yorkshire.

In London, he spent most of his spare time walking alone through the streets and parks, often without any goal.

On those evenings when he had no pressing work to do, he walked for hours, returning very late to his room, exhausted and with blisters on his feet.

John Yeadon had been brought up in a small town in Yorkshire. In a town where men spend most of their lives working under the earth.

One of those Yorkshire towns made of endless rows of grey terraced houses, whose treeless streets are always damp and where huge slabs of dark clouds sit permanently over smoking roofs.

His father had been killed in a mining accident. The kind of accident which occurred from time to time, when men perish, alive, under rubble, never to see the light of day again.

For many years after his father died, his mother would rush up the stairs to watch, from the windows of her parlour, the men returning to their houses.

When her husband was alive she used to smile and wave to him from the parlour as she saw him arriving with the other miners.

In John Yeadon's home town the social life took place in the local pub.

Each Friday and Saturday, women from nearby towns who had fallen on hard times performed stripteases, accompanied by bands made up of unemployed local lads.

On these occasions, the pub would be packed with miners and their wives. After the pub closed, the fish and chip shop just across the street became the centre of attention.

The customers streamed out of the pub and went to form a queue outside the chippy. Some asked for cod and chips, others fish-cakes and chips, yet others asked for sausages and chips, which they sprinkled with salt and vinegar. Then they walked through the bare streets in twos and threes towards their houses, leaving behind a strong trail of hot vinegar.

In the early mornings, discarded portions of fish and chips could be seen scattered on wet pavements.

As a teenager he had felt he was a stranger to this life, and instead of going to the pub, he used to spend his evenings studying for his exams and dreaming of going to London to study accountancy and working in a bank.

To keep himself informed, he went to the local library to read the financial pages of the Yorkshire Post.

At the end of his accountancy course he found a job almost immediately. He started as a junior clerk with one of the big banks and was attached to their main branch in the City.

After several promotions and after three years of saving he managed, with the help of his bank's mortgage facilities, to move out of the room in King's Cross and bought a one bedroom flat in Boxhill, Surrey.

After he bought the flat, his mother, delighted that her son was now settling into a place of his own, came down for ten days to help him to furnish it.

In fact, as he himself had no idea of what he did or did not like, his mother chose everything for him.

She said she would furnish it in homely Yorkshire style so that in the evenings it would remind him of home.

She had it carpeted with a pink and brown floral pattern and the walls were papered with bright floral motifs. The curtains matched the wallpaper and the net curtains were decorated with lace she'd made herself in Yorkshire.

The settee was covered in sky-blue velvet, which she told him was his father's favourite colour. On the walls, she hung pictures of floral bouquets and a view of Ripon Cathedral, all in richly gilded frames.

The flat had a small, if rather windswept, balcony overlooking Boxhill station. (He'd bought his flat close to the station so that it would be easy for him to go to work very early in the morning.)

She remembered that her son had once said to her that he liked marigolds. So she bought several flower boxes from the local garden centre and filled them with plastic marigolds.

"When spring comes", she told him that evening, "you replace them with fresh ones.

Then in the autumn, when the fresh marigolds die, you take the dead ones out, wash the plastic marigolds and put them back in the boxes.

That way you'll have the nice-looking yellow colour of the marigolds on the balcony all year around. But remember to wash the plastic marigolds under the tap every time you take them out."

And so for the next twenty years, each spring and each winter John Yeadon followed his mother's advice and replaced the marigolds from the boxes.

She told him how proud his father would have been to see him settled in a good job and in a brand new flat.

To celebrate his new home and thank his mother for all the work she'd put in, he decided he would take her for tea at Fortnum & Mason, in Piccadilly, that Saturday.

(This was a rather bold financial step for him after all the expenses incurred with the new flat. Yet, he knew it would please her for she had once told him on the phone that she'd read about Fortnum & Mason in her paper and learned that the smart London ladies went there for tea.)

He meant to go ahead with his idea, irrespective of the expense — although he knew well that he would have to make savings later.

She was delighted and on that day she made a special effort to look as much of a lady as possible.

She wore a dress she'd worn only on a few occasions together with the pair of black shoes she'd worn only at her husband's funeral. Over the neck of her coat she'd put on a loose strip of fur.

After her son went to work — for he often liked to go to the office on Saturday when the bank was closed to catch up with his paperwork — she went, without telling him, to the hairdresser and had her silver hair done, "in the latest fashion for a lady of my age".

Before going out of the flat that early afternoon she put a fresh coat of red lipstick on her white lips. When she went to the bathroom to look at herself in the mirror she was struck by the sharp, sharp contrast of her luxuriantly red lips against her white face,

A face white as death itself.

They had arranged to meet outside the Jermyn Street entrance of Fortnum & Mason at 4.30 p.m.. She was anxious not to be late and she arrived fifteen minutes early. She took a brief stroll along Jermyn Street to look at the windows of the elegant shops.

He arrived, rushing, ten minutes late and, pretending not to recognise his mother in her new hairstyle and smart clothes, went straight inside the restaurant.

She went after him murmuring:

"Johnny, Johnny, dear.
It's Mum, Johnny.
It's Mum."

He'd booked a table in a position that would give her a good view of the large and splendid room full of people. Once they sat at their table, she looked in wonder at the general decor of the room, the chandeliers, the carpets, the china, the frescoed walls, the elegant ladies...

After a while, her son had to shake her gently to say that tea had arrived. She looked at what was laid in front of her with utter amazement.

She saw the many-tiered silver cake-stand with all sorts of exquisitely cut and presented sandwiches, decorative vegetables made in the form of flowers, many varieties of delightful cakes, white and brown scones, jams and creams, the beautiful rose-patterned china and the silver crockery incised with floral motifs...

Then, turning to her son, she whispered:

"I wish your father had lived to see this day".

And as she uttered these words her eyelids started to flutter, as if in an attempt to hide her now moistened eyes.

IV

In the subsequent twenty-two years that he was to spend in London, he went to see his mother up in Yorkshire every third weekend of the month. He would take the six o'clock train from King's Cross on a Friday night straight after work and arrive at his mother's house at about nine.

By the time he arrived, she would have a hot meal ready for him.

On Sundays they'd go together to church. She had got roast beef with Yorkshire pudding ready for lunch and plenty of cooked vegetables.

As she got older he spent most of the weekend there making sure her little affairs were in good order — that the lawn had been mown, the roses pruned, the bills paid, the roof not leaking.

On her eightieth birthday she had come to London and he had taken her for tea once again to Fortnum & Mason.

Once a year, usually in July, he would take her for a ten-day holiday to the Lake District. They had been going there since he'd been a child, for his father used to rent a caravan and together they went walking over the hills and the wild moors.

Now they stayed in a bed and breakfast near where his father used to take them.

After his father died, thinking that she might find the same place painful, he had suggested to her that they might take their holiday in Morecambe, where there were more people and where they could walk along the seafront.

"No, no," she answered,
"we must keep going there.
Father liked it there.
We must keep father's spirit alive,
however painful that is."

In fact after several holidays there they both found it less and less difficult and instead of experiencing a sense of disquiet they felt reassured by their memories.

During their walks, which became shorter and shorter with her advancing age, she often repeated comments her husband had made to her about a certain view, a lake, a stream, a wood.

As she became older she came to depend on him more and more. They would telephone each other four or five times each week. She did most of the talking and was happy to know that her son was at the other end of the line listening.

Sometimes he would quietly put the telephone on the settee and continue with his little jobs around the flat and as he heard her saying

"Johnny, Johnny.
 Are you listening?" He would go back and say,
"Mum, of course I am listening".

Then, as she kept repeating herself, he would say to her:

"Now you are tired.
It's late, Mum.
You must go to bed early and sleep in case the neighbour's dogs waken you again in the middle of the night.
Look after yourself.
Good night."

After they parted he would go to the kitchen to make himself a cup of hot chocolate and drink it, slowly, while watching the Ten O'Clock news on ITV.

Before going to bed he went out to his balcony to take a breath of fresh air and look at the yellow marigolds.

By eleven he was fast asleep in his bed.

V

His radio alarm turned itself on at 5.45am and by 6.20 a.m. he would be waiting at the empty station, ready to catch the 6.30 a.m. train.

He much preferred going early to his office to avoid the rush-hour crowds and so have about an hour to himself before his colleagues arrived.

(On the few occasions he had travelled at rush hour the crowds had created a sense of anguish in him and he had arrived at his office full of anxiety.)

On his way to work he normally had a small compartment all to himself and, once he'd made sure that the window was ajar so that fresh air circulated inside, he would take the small flask from his briefcase and pour himself a cup of hot coffee, already with milk and sugar, which he'd prepared the night before.

Then he would spread his papers neatly over the seats and, while sipping his coffee, he would start working. When he arrived at the bank the only people present were three very large, friendly West Indian women who cleaned the offices.

They wore highly patterned, colourful clothes and as they saw him arriving they greeted him with big, big smiles.

At his office he read the mail and dictated his letters into a small tape recorder for the secretary to type later. Sometimes he could hear in the distance the three women singing melancholy songs in their own dialect.

In this way the weeks, the months and the years had gone smoothly by for him. And on that drizzling late October night, while he was sitting at the top of the red bus on his way to the Soho café, he looked absently at the busy streets below.

Then he realised that he'd worked at the bank for exactly twenty-two years and, if he included the one year he'd been a student, he had been making that same journey to the café for precisely twenty-three years.

VI

The journey from the City to Piccadilly Circus lasted about forty-five minutes and he would arrive at the café at 5.15pm.

He always sat at the same long table, at the far end corner of the room, past the glass counter with all the cakes.

He liked to sit at that particular table because it wasn't draughty and because it gave him a good, general view of the whole bustling atmosphere.

Once there he removed his raincoat and put it on the nearest coathanger. Then, he would go to the Gents to refresh himself.

Once at his table he tried to catch the attention of one the ever-changing waitresses, who came from places such as Colombia, Brazil, Venezuela, Portugal and Spain.

He always ordered the same things — a pot of tea, together with a portion of hot buttered toast and blackberry jam.

Although he liked the look of the various éclairs, mille-feuilles, gateaux, tarts, profiteroles, flans and trifles, by nature he did not have, as the English say, a "sweet tooth", so he was content to have his four slices of brown buttered toast.

That evening, as he looked at the mostly changed faces of the customers and at the new decor of the café, he was overwhelmed by a sense of sadness.

As he started sipping his tea he recalled the original owner of the café, a second-generation Italian with a huge belly, a permanently flushed face and pickled eyes. He had then sold the café to another-second generation Italian, a crafty and flamboyant businessman.

In the same district he owned several Italian restaurants, a stand-only bar where immigrant Italians went for their espresso and to watch Italian football matches on a huge screen, a travel agency, a Chinese restaurant and, so the rumour went, several porn shops.

Unlike the old owner, whose café had been the focus of his life for well over forty years and the place where he spent most of his life, the new owner was hardly ever seen by the customers and from the start had appointed a manager who had all sorts of ideas about "improving" the café to reflect the changing character of Soho.

The old owner could in fact have kept working in his café for at least another five years, if he had wished, for he was a man of about sixty and in very good health. But he made up his mind to sell his beloved café after his head waitress, who had worked in the café for thirty years, reached retirement age.

She had always wanted to return to her native Colombia where she had a couple of married daughters and many grown-up grandchildren.

To all her customers she had been known as Dolores, although her full name was Maria Dolorosa.

She always had a stern and stony expression on her face and solid slabs for cheeks.

Her fuzzy hair was chestnut-grey and on her upper lip she had a thin moustache. Her eyes were crossed, her sight very poor, making it necessary for her to wear very thick spectacles which, with her constant running around the café, made her sweat and kept sliding down her thick nose.

In all the years she had been working at the café she had never smiled nor ever once been polite to any of her devoted customers. She even kept the owner firmly in his place, behind the counter. Nobody ever dared to question the way she ran the café.

As the customers arrived she went to their tables and, pretending not to notice them, she would say in her heavily accented English:

"Wat do you vont?"

If they tried to deviate, even slightly, from the set things which the café had always served, she would rudely tell them that they were in the wrong place and should go somewhere else.

Faced with her total indifference, at times, a customer, who was not acquainted with her character, walked straight out of the café, offended.

In the late afternoons, especially if it was raining outside, the café would get extremely crowded. The customers were squeezed shoulder to shoulder along the simple wooden tables.

Sometimes a customer furtively tried to get a chair from another table if a friend had unexpectedly arrived. Before making such a move he'd checked that Dolores was looking away. But, as if she also had hidden eyes behind her massive dark hair, suddenly her frightening voice could be heard from the other end of the room:

"No!, No!", she shouted,
"You can't do det!
You can't.
It not possible.
Each table have the right number of chairs."

Then, pointing with her twisted finger at the table
where the chair was, she'd order the customer to take the
chair back to where it had been.

She terrorised the young waitresses, many of whom did
not last for more than a month. She often humiliated
them in front of all the customers if they did something
which she did not approve of or if they dropped
something on the floor.

On one occasion a poor young Spanish girl, who had
appeared to everyone, including the owner, a good, well-
intentioned girl, broke down in tears after being
humiliated once too often.

She dropped the tray of teas and cakes and, collapsing
on the floor, she sobbed and trembled as large tears
flooded out of her tender, black eyes.

Many of the people rushed to calm her down, but to no
avail.

For the first time in the long history of the café
everybody noticed a slight tinge of remorse pass through
Dolores' normally rock-solid face — as if on that
occasion she'd recognised that perhaps she'd gone too
far.

Yet, despite her hardness and sometimes downright
cruelty towards the young waitresses, her regular
customers, who were by now mostly in their mid-fifties,
had come to love her for what she was.

They simply could not imagine what the café could be
like without her. She had become an essential part of the
place. Indeed the place was how it was because of her,
that is

unchanged for over forty years,
with the same old brown tables,
the same bare, smoky walls which were once apricot,

the same manual till behind the counter which
at times simply would not open,
the same huge wedding cake in the window and
that same yellowed, beaded veil against it.

Every time that the good-natured owner had suggested any change to her she had twisted her face unpleasantly with total disapproval.

And he, poor man, would never have dared to do anything without her consent.

The result was that everything stayed the same, year after year, decade after decade.

The affection in which she had been held was shown by the fact that when the time of her retirement came the customers decided to bid farewell to her on her last day at the café with a surprise party.

The organisers, with the support of the owner, had arranged for a big cake to be made in the colours and shape of her native Colombia. Using varied Colombian coffee beads and confetti they had inscribed the following words:

"Dolores, we love you.
We shall all miss you.
Happy retirement from all the faithfuls."

The candles on the cake represented all the years she had worked at the café.

On her last day, at around 5.30 p.m., when the café was packed with all the faithfuls, the lights of the café went off suddenly. The people who did not know of the secret party, and also Dolores herself, thought of a power cut.

A few moments later, to the amazement of Dolores, from the utter darkness of the staircase emerged a man dressed all in white. He held a big cake shaped like her beloved native Colombia, covered with small flickering candles.

As he came down the stairs the corks from several bottles of champagne started exploding and the lights were at the same time switched on, revealing a flood of affectionate smiles directed towards Dolores.

As soon as she read the inscription on the cake a smile lit up her face as tears ran down her mellowed cheeks.

That was the first time in her thirty years at the café that she'd been seen smiling and without the stony expression on her face. The first time she'd shown she had tender feelings within herself.

VII

A year after her retirement the owner decided that without Dolores in charge of the café he couldn't keep it going. He soon realised that he could not keep control over his staff who started to demand large pay increases which the café could not afford and threatened him with strikes and sit-ins.

They wanted more paid holidays, fewer working hours and better working conditions. They even demanded that their season tickets be paid for by the café.

As soon as the various suppliers heard of Dolores's retirement they started to be more difficult every day. They shortened their normal credit facilities and demanded to be paid earlier while at the same time increasing the prices of their goods.

He was too soft-hearted to resist any of their demands. Everybody, of course, knew that he'd relied entirely on Dolores's iron approach and now they took full advantage of her absence.

He realised how necessary the hard heart of Dolores had been in order to survive in the cut-throat commercial world of Soho.

So he decided to sell and accepted the low figure offered by the astute Soho businessman, who had obviously been briefed about the old owner's weaknesses.

The first signs of the new management came one day when, to the shock of the old regulars, they found that the walls, which had not been painted for forty years, had been redone in a dazzling white.

A week later they suffered another shock when they discovered that "pictures" had been placed on the walls, walls which had been bare since the café had opened in the late forties.

The "pictures", which had gilded frames, were bad copies of well-known French impressionist paintings done by students from a nearby art school and depicted scenes of café society in Paris at the turn of the century.

The third shock came when the original wooden cakes counter was replaced with an unfriendly-looking high-tech counter which controlled the temperature automatically.

The ancient till had been held in particular affection by all the customers because of the charming bell noise it made every time it was opened as well as for its unpredictable nature. Now it was cruelly replaced by an unfriendly electronic till which assumed that people were innumerate, telling the waitresses what change to give to customers.

The greatest shock of all came when both the huge wedding cake and the yellow beaded veil against the window were taken away and the whole window made new.

Then it was the turn of the dark wooden floor which was replaced with a fake marble one.

As these major changes occurred many of the old customers, instead of protesting, stopped going to the café.

That late October evening as John Yeadon sat in the café despondently looking at the changes he wondered why he was still going there.

Many of the customers were a new breed of people among whom he felt alien.

They consisted of noisy, youngish, arty people working in film, television, radio, advertising, production and record companies. The overheard conversations were now mostly focused on contracts, co-productions, sponsorship, community programming, equal opportunities for single mothers and blacks in television and so on.

Yet despite his hurt feelings about the ways things had developed in the café he still felt a strong urge to go there day after day.

He considered the idea of going to another café but could not think of another which he liked.

The thought of going straight home after work at that early hour (as his colleagues did) had somehow always filled him with dismay.

He immediately thought of the suffocating rush hour crowds, the traffic jams, the noise, the train delays and cancellations, the hour-long stand and squeeze on the train, the long pauses in the dark tunnels while the train waited for the lines to clear...

Then once he was at home what would he do until he went to bed at eleven? He had never liked to spend hours watching television like his colleagues. Then, as he started to count the hours he had to fill before going to bed, he felt an overwhelming sense of despair.

He came to the realisation that the two and a half hours he'd spent at the café for the last twenty-three years, hours in which he had simply been happy just to look, anonymously,

at the people coming and going,
browsing through the newspapers,
drinking his tea,
asking for a little more hot water
as the evening progressed,
eating his buttered toast with blackberry jam,
glancing occasionally at the stony-faced Dolorcs,
feeling sorry for the poor young waitresses, and at
times looking at the pickled-eyed owner behind the
counter...

all this had come to be an essential part of his daily life.

VIII

That late October evening he left the café, sadly, at the usual time of 7.30 p.m. and walked through the cold, drizzling winter's night towards Charing Cross station in time to catch his train to Boxhill, Surrey.

As he walked through the crowded streets of Soho, lit by the coloured neon lights of the theatres, restaurants, pubs, porno shops, brasseries... large groups of people were gathering in front of the theatres.

Small groups of Japanese, Italian, Scandinavian and American tourists roamed curiously through the streets. The occasional pin-striped businessman could be seen looking around before going in to see a prostitute. Men and women tried to entice passing businessmen to go and see their topless shows...

While he strolled he remembered the time when prostitutes, who used to occupy the rooms above the café, had thrown freshly-used condoms at the respectable people passing below in the street. As they saw their reactions they threw themselves with great laughter onto the beds where they earned their living.

He recalled the time when young prostitutes used to go to him to ask whether he wanted a "rubber glove manipulation", which he had always declined, but without ever having discovered what they had actually meant by it.

He recalled the occasions in the café when, sitting at the crowded table, he had felt his leg being brushed but had not been able to decide if it came from the man or woman sitting opposite him.

As he continued to stroll he noticed that the whole character of Soho itself was dramatically changing since the council had started a clean-up campaign. Many of the old porn shops were slowly being replaced by expensive boutiques catering for the new young, arty crowds who now frequented the café. The prostitutes were also being ruthlessly pushed out of Soho and their rooms were being turned into offices for the media world.

As he was about to cross Leicester Square he saw an old woman tramp whose smiling face reminded him of the sweet old lady who used to arrive every afternoon at the café in her chauffeur-driven car and whose name he only discovered after her death when an obituary appeared in a national newspaper.

She too used always to sit at the same table not far from him and, with her bird-like little mouth, used to order tea and a strawberry flan. He had once overheard her saying proudly, just a few months before her death, that she had been coming to the same café for thirty-five years.

She was a bubbly lady, always cheerful, and often giggled like a young girl. She'd arrive every day wearing a different hat. She must have had a very large collection of these colourful, feathery hats for the other customers could never tell whether the one she was wearing on any particular day had already been seen by them.

She had died only a few months before the retirement party for Dolores. Had she survived, she would have undoubtedly played a major role in its planning.

The news of her death was broken to them a few days later by her uniformed chauffeur who arrived one day at the café without her.

As they heard the news of her death the skin on their faces dropped, heavily, in the way the curtains drop at a West End theatre after a very disappointing performance.

A few days later the obituary appeared in the paper, accompanied by a large photograph of her wearing one of her most outrageous hats and her unmistakable grin on her face. The photograph had, in fact, been taken by a famous thirties photographer.

From the article the customers learned that she had been a leading society lady of the twenties and thirties and to the delight of all the article also had a paragraph about her long-standing association with her favourite Soho café.

When he reached the long narrow street by Saint Martin-in-the-Fields he was confronted by a long row of begging, homeless people, both young and old, women and children, while in the distance a young student busker played a poignant fragment from one of Bach's cello suites.

As he was about to go down the passageway he noticed an old man standing behind a glowing brazier urging passersby, in a strong Irish voice, to try his roasted chestnuts.

The chestnut seller's voice immediately reminded him of the old drunken Irish painter whose works, so rumour went inside the café, sold at Bond Street auctions for millions of pounds.

He too had become part of the fabric of the café. He sat every day at his table, often very noisily, talking to himself, making loud burps, sometimes annoying the old lady by stealing and then wearing one of her eccentric hats.

He recalled the painter arriving one evening at the café, totally drunk and barely able to walk. He arrived carrying a small canvas under his right arm. Somehow he managed to step on to his chair and from there on to the table, crushing with one of his feet a tray full of cream gateaux.

And as he leaned against the sticky and smoky wall he asked all the people in the café to look at his canvas. It depicted the upper part of a disfigured man standing in front of a marble counter. Behind the marble counter hung a large carcass of meat still dripping with blood. Above the disfigured man's head there was a big, dimly-lit bulb.

A few moments later, while pointing with his right hand at the picture, he shouted, in an incoherent, drunken voice:

"This is me.
It's me at the butcher's.
I finished it today.
Would anyone like to buy it?
I'm broke.
Broke.
Please buy it.
I'm broke, broke."

Then, with his shoulders against the wall he started to slide down on to the table, creating chaos inside the café as cups, pots and cakes were scattered all over the floor.

That was one of the very few occasions when Dolores had somehow managed to let things get out of her control.

The drunken painter had also died, just a few months before the eccentric former society lady and about six months before Dolores's retirement.

The painter's body was discovered, one early December morning, in a narrow Soho lane by a group of refuse collectors.

His body lay,
cold, rigid and lifeless,
amid a pile of rubbish bags,
encircled by
a wreath of dead winter leaves.

In the stiff fist of his right hand was, trapped, the neck of an almost empty bottle of whisky.

The glare of the neon lights
    Flushed upon his frosted eyes,
And below his frosted eyes there were
    Dew drops, caught
In the bitter sting of the night.

IX

By the time John Yeadon arrived at Charing Cross station the rush hour crowds had gone.

The station was now quiet but an air of exhaustion permeated the whole building.

The vast granite floor was conspicuous by its black stains while the litter bins overflowed with debris.

He'd gone to sit, as usual, in an empty compartment near the front of the train. A few minutes later, however, three other passengers had entered the compartment.

A middle-aged woman, with tousled grey hair, sat opposite him wearing a black raincoat and a very tight belt just below her breasts. Her eyes, greatly enlarged by her thick glasses, had a staring quality.

At the other end of the compartment two men in business suits, a young and an older man, sat opposite each other.

Everybody studiously avoided looking at the other passengers in the compartment; nor did anyone, in any way, acknowledge the presence of the other people.

The two men in business suits started to browse through the evening paper, the middle-aged woman with magnified eyes pulled out of her bag a romantic paperback which she started to read.

As the train emerged from the station to plunge into the rainy darkness of the night, John D. Yeadon, still immersed in his memories of the Soho café, looked sadly, through the rain-splashed window, at the melting London lights.

*

The Coolness of England
(A fragment)

I

Then ... spring arrived. The days started to get brighter and less rainy. In late April Anthony succeeded in taking ten days off from his busy job in the City. Six months earlier, soon after his thirty-eighth birthday, the legal firm where he worked had made him a partner.

On several occasions during that winter he had said we should visit Cornwall together. He wanted to show me the places associated with his childhood. He had talked of the beauty of the Cornish countryside in springtime when the fields are full of wild flowers, the air is at its freshest and it is the time when the Atlantic winds start to get less cold. The birdsongs and the foliage in the countryside are at their best and the walks over the cliffs in the broad bay are exhilarating.

With some difficulty I also arranged to take time off work. (I had only recently left the University of Urbino and was then a young man starting my first job with an Italian firm in London.) Very early one rainy morning we left London behind and drove down on the motorway towards Cornwall. We stayed on the motorway as far as

Bristol. Then, on Anthony's suggestion, we took the winding country roads.

That April day I saw for the first time the undulating landscape of Devon, its sleepy villages and the village greens; the ponds with ducks and swans ... the thatched cottages and pubs. I saw spring meadows smothered in drifts of primulas and snowdrops stirring in the wind. I saw woods with tender leaves and carpets of bluebells.

II

As we drove slowly through the countryside, the changing light and pattern of clouds was a constant source of delight. One moment a field would be illuminated brightly by the sun. A moment later, the same field would be immersed in gloomy darkness. Then a beam of sunlight would fall on a cluster of old oak trees by a hillside. Then ... it would rain again. A rainbow would suddenly appear and link the opposite sides of a valley.

As we got deeper and deeper into the countryside and closer and closer to North Cornwall it felt as if a mantle of coolness fell upon us.

We reached the border between Devon and Cornwall at about four in the afternoon. We came across a small village and decided to stop for a rest. There was a little hotel in the village which overlooked a large pond. There, in front of a burning fireplace, I had my first full English tea with warm scones, blackberry jam, clotted cream and beautifully cut sandwiches.

We had spoken very little during that journey. We were very happy to be with each other. I drove during the stretch of the motorway. Then, when we took the country roads, Anthony took over the driving. My eyes were constantly looking at the ever-changing landscape.

Over tea Anthony started to talk about his family whom I was going to meet that evening. He had warned them that he was bringing an Italian friend. His mother, he told me, was in her late sixties. A few years earlier she had suffered an unusual kind of stroke which had entirely paralysed her face.

The function of her brain and eyes had remained unscathed by the attack but all the muscles on her face had been permanently damaged. The expression on her face, immediately after the stroke, was suddenly frozen and she felt as if she were wearing a mask of granite which she could never take off.

The skin on her face felt dead. She was unable to smile, although, Anthony said, she made great efforts with her eyes. When she washed her face in the morning it was as if she were washing a piece of stone.

Anthony's ex-navy father, on the other hand, who was in his mid-seventies, was in excellent health and led a highly active country life; he looked after his wife very well.

He had an older brother, Anthony continued, who had followed in the footsteps of his father and had become a captain in the Royal Navy. (He was then on a ship in Australia.) He also had a younger sister who had married a visiting American scientist while she was studying at Bristol University. His sister, he said, had never been particularly academic. She didn't finish her degree. When the American returned to take up a professorship in biology in California she had abandoned her course and followed him there. She became a happy housewife and bore her husband three children, they rarely returned to England.

III

It was nearly eight o'clock in the evening and pitch dark when we finally arrived at Anthony's parents' house in North Cornwall.

That day we had been very lucky with the weather. Although there had been huge banks of clouds regularly sweeping across the sky it had rained very little.

We drove down the drive of their house through dark foliage and stopped in front of the house. Anthony's father, in impeccable tweeds, came out to welcome us. When we went inside I saw his wife sitting — expressionless — by the burning fireplace.

On seeing me come into the house she got up and, with her little watery eyes which reflected the warm orange glow of the fireplace, she smiled sweetly — as best she could. She could barely speak.

The loose skin on her white face was deeply furrowed and had the appearance of a ploughed field frozen in the depth of winter. But her little, gooseberry-like eyes, which had slightly sunk inside her skull, sparkled with a warm light.

Her husband's face contrasted very sharply. His cheeks had the colour of mature field cherries and all his body seemed to throb with health and vigour. He had a neatly-kept white moustache.

After supper that evening we went out for a stroll to the little harbour not far from the house. Anthony's mother stayed at home.

The strong sea wind had suddenly cleared the sky of all the clouds. In the gleaming night sky there was a full, bright moon which cast a silver light over the harbour and the countryside.

The village lay in a wooded valley. Most of its white stone cottages had been built along one bank of a fast-flowing stream whose dark waters rippled and played over the shallow stones, filling the dry cold air with the fresh sound of running water.

Ten minutes later we reached the village's enclosed little harbour. A few small fishing boats were moored, tied to big wet, rusty metal knobs on the pier. There was the clanking sound of dangling chains and of boats which, with each oncoming wave, rubbed against each other on the dark waters.

We took the winding path over the black slate cliff. The ground was a little slippery and soaked with water. The air on my face was biting and invigorating.

A few moments later the path emerged onto a wide ledge; and from this ledge on the huge cliff I saw the wide open sea — moonlit and with a silver sheen. It lay vast and smooth, placid and immense in front of my eyes. Its waters shimmered in the moonlight; and the sky, the sky was a gleaming dark immensity of bright stars and constellations.

That first night in Cornwall I slept well. The long, meandering journey and the country air undoubtedly contributed to this. The following morning I was woken by the smell of frying bacon which came slowly into my room. I got out of bed. I drew the curtains and opened the window. Fresh sea air flooded into my room. I looked outside. The newly-leafed shrubs and trees were moving in the sea wind.

The sky was overcast and grey. Large thick layers of clouds scurried over a subdued, green and sombre landscape. In the distance there was a meadow with clusters of wild daffodils which glowed in the general darkness of the morning. Beyond the meadow there was a hill with a silver birch wood.

I heard the screeching noise of seagulls coming from the harbour. The image of fishermen's boats returning from an all-night fishing trip came into my mind.

When I went downstairs into the sitting room the smell of bacon permeated everything. It was just before eight. The radio was on. Anthony's father was busy in the kitchen getting the table ready for breakfast. His wife was cooking in the kitchen. Anthony came into the sitting room looking happy. He asked if I had slept well. Then there was a knock at the door and he went to open it. A boy of about twelve handed him a copy of the *Daily Telegraph.*

As we were having breakfast I felt a little embarrassed and uncomfortable. I've never liked to be the centre of attention. Anthony's parents were quite good. They didn't bombard me with questions, which would have happened if I had been in an equivalent Italian situation. I was relieved by this. In the natural daylight, the effects of the stroke on Anthony's mother seemed more disquieting. Her eyes were small, gentle and sweet. The father's cheeks seemed redder and his moustache even whiter.

IV

After breakfast Anthony wanted to show me his favourite childhood places. We first walked along the village stream and looked at the white stone cottages along the bank. We went to look at the old village pub with its slate floor and austere, monastic feel. We went up the narrow cobbled streets over the hill. We walked into the village's only hotel which had once been the local manor house, its walls still covered with old family portraits.

We then walked for about half an hour through the wood, along the bank of the stream. The path climbed over the valley covered with birch trees on both sides. The ground under the trees was full of white garlic flowers and their strong scent permeated the moist air.

The wood was full of the sound of birds and tumbling water. Later it started to rain but the leaves on the trees prevented us from getting wet. After a while the rain stopped and bright rays of sunlight began to seep through the new leaves. The sun created mottled patterns of light on the dark brown stream waters, over the masses of garlic flowers and on the leaves of the shrubs.

Inside the wood there were slanting and vertical rays of sunlight illuminating the silver bark of the birches. On both sides of the stream banks I saw delicate primroses of great freshness and beauty. Everything in that wood looked luxuriant and alive. The trees, the water, the flowers, the new foliage, the air, everything was moist, green and fresh. It was like being in the very heart of nature.

Later the path emerged into the open hills and fields. On the brow of a hill, in the distance, I saw a small cluster of old trees. Nestled amongst these trees were the stones of an ancient church. Its solid tower jutted into the constantly moving sky. "That", Anthony said, "is the church we often walked to when I was a child. Isn't it lovely?" The sight, from where we stood, was indeed most charming. It was a pure rural idyll, like a little poem by Virgil.

When we reached the cluster of trees surrounding the church, we came to a fence of barbed wire which we couldn't cross. For a while we walked around in search of an entrance.

We found the wooden gate at the other side of the field which took us into a well-kept churchyard covered with medieval slate headstones. Many were cracked and peeling, while others were leaning against an old brick wall and covered with ivy. Amongst the headstones there was a tall weathered Celtic cross over which a wild honeysuckle had climbed. Several of the old graves had clumps of wild daffodils and primulas growing in the crevices.

All this was inside a cluster of trees — oaks, junipers and yews — which had protected the site from centuries of sea wind, hail and rain.

On one side of the church entrance was an old yew tree, darkly monumental, brooding and melancholy. The interior of the church had a great simplicity. The massive bare structure of the walls dominated the little space inside. The rows of dark wooden pews, which were streaked by fleeting rays of sunlight, appeared shy. There was an ancient baptismal font of black marble.

We climbed the narrow stairs to the top of the solid square tower. From there we saw beautiful views.

On one side there was the vast expanse of the ocean with the massive clouds which sailed above it. On the other side, in the distance, beyond some green fields, there was the immense desolation of the moor, which looked like a city afflicted by perpetual sorrow; and there the rain was falling down like tears from the sky.

V

On Sunday afternoon we visited an Elizabethan house, set deep in the countryside amongst old oaks, beeches, chestnuts and flowering rhododendrons. The house was still lived in by the owners, and visitors were allowed to visit only its walled gardens and the parkland around the house.

When we arrived an elderly gentleman, looking very much like a retired army officer, handed us a guide which included a plan and description of each "room" of the walled garden.

We entered the garden and the first room. "This room", the notes read, "is devoted to the May-flowering blackthorn. Each spring its black branches give birth to the loveliest of white petals which completely cover the branches and always appear before the leaves. They give the feeling of newly fallen snow. If the flowering of the blackthorn coincides with a spell of bitterly cold wind, in these parts we speak of a 'Blackthorn Winter'."

From the blackthorn room we then walked into another room. "This room", the notes went on say, "is devoted to the sweet briar, originally a wild English rose. It blossoms each year in early spring. When it blossoms it fills the room with the joyous glory of an English spring. Both its leaves and petals are sweetly fragrant; every time there is a sea breeze the air becomes filled with its scent."

We saw several other rooms and then we strolled in the park which surrounded the house.

There were avenues of flowering azaleas and rhododendrons and drifts of orange, scarlet, white and purple flowers which glowed against the shiny dark-green foliage of the shrubs underneath a heavy and overcast sky. Every time the wind stirred the azaleas and rhododendrons, the colours of the flowers seemed to assume different hues. Some of the flowers darkened while others got brighter ...

*

II
Poems

*...And I from the first signs of a lovely dawn
can never cease to sigh while there is light,*

*Then when I see the flickering of the stars
I start to weep and long for the gone day.*

Petrarch

My Religion
In Memoriam B.A.J.
(1939-1990)

I

It was on a fine, clear day in the spring of 1978 that Anthony and I first met.

He had then fair hair with silvery touches above his ears.

His beautiful blue eyes seized me with a gentle force.

On that spring day we strolled in the rose garden of Regent's Park.

A sweet scent was in the air.

The roses were beginning to burst out of their buds and the leaves had a fresh, shining tenderness.

The honeysuckle around the rose garden was in full flower.

The inner-circle path was lined, on both sides, by young cherry trees, all in full blossom.

Whilst we were strolling that spring afternoon, Anthony and I realised that a live current connected our bodies. A current which was to be extinguished twelve years later.

II

During our years together, our love, like all loves, went through changes.

The sensuousness of the early years mellowed and developed into affection and devotion.

We spent many holidays together mainly in North Cornwall and in the Highlands of Scotland where, during our long walks, we felt the unjudging powers of nature touch our bodies, just as the cold winds invigorated our minds.

We took joy in each other's achievements.

I remember vividly the loving light in his smiling eyes when I told him in hospital that I had been awarded my doctorate. He had just fallen ill.

He opened his weakened arms.

He embraced me.

Tears moistened his eyes.

He nodded to the nurses to bring the chilled bottle of champagne which he had ordered earlier that day.

I brought a glass to his mouth, but the champagne could freshen only his drying lips.

I understood the tears in his eyes for he had read every word of my thesis, looked at every lapse of style, discussed with me every idea behind the text.

III

From our love we both derived power and strength.

Through our love the once reserved, timorous side of Anthony developed into self-respect and pride.

The Anthony of the earlier years hesitating to take me to a promenade concert for fear his career might suffer later became for both of us a complete stranger.

During the hours, days, weeks and months of his illness, our relationship grew ever stronger.

Our love experienced a new spring.

We savoured each other's every breath.
Our bodies were drawn to each other as never before.
He seemed more beautiful every day.
We comforted each other.
Occasionally, we sobbed in each other's arms.
Throughout his illness he was always the stronger.
He accepted the imminence of his death with tranquillity.
And never felt self-pity.
But he knew that I would be left on my own, without him.
He knew that my flesh was sewn to his.
(I adored him.)
He knew how anguished I was when he was away, if only
for a few days.
He knew I wanted to go wherever he went, to stay
wherever he stayed. To sleep wherever he slept.
He knew the importance of his late-night calls to me when
he was working abroad.
Knew I could not sleep without hearing his voice.
He knew how I loved hearing him read before we turned
off the bedroom lights.
Knew he was my loved one, my only one.
He consoled me.
With infinite tenderness.

IV

In his last weeks, he became weaker.
It was spring again.
We went to Regent's Park every day.
I held his arm firmly in mine. We walked, gently, again
like two young lovers, through the rose garden.
The days were clear and sunny.
Whenever we sat on a bench, the cool morning breeze
would blow the petals from the cherry blossoms onto our
clothes.
The sky had the colour of his eyes.
Then came the relapse.

He lost weight. I drove him to hospital.
He stayed there for a month.
I saw him getting worse every day.
He couldn't eat.
His eyes had sunk.
His cheeks hollowed.
I saw a shadow of death lingering beneath his skin.
I became frightened.
I said I would take him home again.
The next day, he was home.

In that month our house had lost all interest for me. I had neglected everything.

I had taken no pleasure in looking at our herb garden. I had not cut the grass nor watered the plants.

In the sitting room, a vase of white roses withered. I had found every excuse to be out of the house.

Once he was back, a light seemed again to seep into our house.

We sat and read to each other in the garden. I replaced the withered roses.

We both inspected the plants. I cut the grass, watered the plants. Anthony watched and approved.

Each day I gave him fruit and milk drinks. They nourished him.

I blended them for a long time until they achieved the silkiest of textures.

Sometimes I had to force him, gently. It was painful for both of us.

His throat, like his lungs, had wounds.
He would cough.
He would hold my hand.
Then we would try again.
I would kiss him.
He would smile.

V

Anthony made a remarkable recovery.
He smiled again.

His cheeks filled out.

The following week we were walking again in the rose garden.

The roses were in full bloom.

As we passed the banks filled with different scents and colours, he talked eagerly of those he liked and those he didn't.

But his recovery was not to last.

Two weeks later he began to feel breathless.

He grew weak again.

His cheeks hollowed.

His face was moist with sweat and now shone with a waxy pallor.

I saw once more a shadow of death lingering beneath his pale skin.

I held him tight.

We went back to hospital.

There, the nurses gave him an oxygen mask. The doctors told me that his lungs were bleeding.

I kissed him.

I wiped the sweat from his face with a scented cloth. His breathing eased.

He looked at me with a faint smile.

One hour before he went into a coma, he saw my distressed eyes.

With trembling arms he drew my head to his chest.

I heard his laboured breathing.

The slow beats of his heart.

The rumbling of bleeding lungs.

He held my head against his chest and caressed my hair, as he had done every night.

His hands were marked, wounded by the repeated punctures into his veins.

VI

The most beautiful moment in his illness was when, for
the first time, I could wash him in a warm bath.
I embraced that moment.
He had grown too weak.
I washed every part of his body.
I tickled, tweaked and kissed him.
He smiled.
I washed, I cut his hair. Clipped his toe nails.
I wrapped his body in a warm towel.
I laid him on our bed, where our bare bodies had slept
intertwined for all those years.
I dried him, gently. I looked at him.
His eyes had a clear freshness of spring.
I touched his weary body, the temple of my desires.
I kissed every inch of his body as I inhaled its
unmistakable fragrance.
During these moments, a strange peace reigned
between us.
Then, I realised that Anthony had been
my lover,
my friend,
my brother,
my father.
I realised that I had come to worship him.
I realised that he had become my religion.

*

*Read by the author at the BBC Memorial Celebration of
Anthony Jennings' life held in St James Church, Piccadilly,
London on Monday 25th June 1990.*

The Deep Heart Of Spring
(After Gyodai, 1732–1793)

The willows hang down in the shadows,

The cherry-blossoms float
  Whitely in the twilight.

Gradually, it darkens.
  A soft breeze rises and

The sound of water alone is heard.

I sit on the verandah,
  Gazing at the distant hills, they

Slowly fade into the dusk.

In all this there is the deep heart of spring.

Spring Love

The morning coolness of the valley
  The sweet sound of the chilled waters

The running stream

The moist brown earth of the grave
  The luminous green waters of

The calm sea

The clear freshness of
  The wild spring flowers

The still fresh spring of love

Rippling Winds

How many dawns were chilled
By the rippling winds

While

A wreath of thorns bloomed
Upon his bloodied head

While

Lost he walked through a field
of white chrysanthemums

The Fiery Dawn
(After Hart Crane)

Your hands within my hands
    Are deeds

My tongue upon your tongue
    Singing

My heart against your heart
    Trembling

Arms close, eyes to eyes
    Mouth to mouth

Drink — The fiery dawn

Hyacinths In the Rain

I

April and a shower of rain
As gulls rush noisily through the air.

Alone in the park
I strolled in the falling rain.

Then, suddenly, through beams of sunlight
And that falling rain

I see my love stand
By the hyacinth blooms.

II

The curls of his hair were dripping with rain.
Cradled in his arms

A cluster of orange-coloured hyacinths
Glow in the rain.

The air is heavy with hyacinth scent.
I call to my love but found I could not speak.

A shower of tears and my eyesight failed.
Beams of sunlight and a shower of rain.

The Memory Of Those Lips

The memory of
   Those lips,

The blue of
   Those eyes,

But now this, lonely,
   Lonely grief.

The Last Blue Mountains

There are those
who walk in darkness

Those who wait for
Love, and despair ...

And there are those
Who gaze

At the last blue mountains
And the calm seashore.

My Loved And I, As One
(After an ancient Japanese poem)

I

I loved him like
The lush leaves of spring
That descend the branches of the willow
Standing on the jutting bank

Where we two walked together
While he was still of this world

My life was built on him
(Yet one cannot flout
The laws of this world)

II

To the wide fields where
The heat haze shimmers
Hidden in a white cloud
He soared like the morning bird

Hidden from our world
like the setting sun
I lifted him, high into the sky
I clasped him firmly into my arms

III

By the pillows where we lay
My Loved And I, As One
The daylight I now pass lonely

'Till dusk
    The black night I lie sighing
'Till dawn

I grieve
    Yet know of no remedy
I pine
    Yet know of no way of meeting him

The Flowers That Were His Eyes
(After Gerard Manley Hopkins)

L ovely in limbs,
    Lovely in eyes ...

The flowers
    That were his eyes.

Satie and the Bat

S ad irony
    At the break of dawn

The jewels in the mountains
    The orange colours

And the break of dawn

The dance of the bat
    To the music of Satie

In the rustic room overlooking
    The jewels in the mountains

That Early Morning in May

I

That early morning in May...
   The day had just begun to break.
In the garden the daffodils
  Glowed in the grey morning light.

On the chestnut the spring leaves
  Were enveloped in the damp, misty air.
My case stood by the door and a
  Chilled air slipped in from the street.

II

That early morning in May...
   My grieving heart was dark as night.
Then, I entered the drizzling rain,
  Walked the amber-lighted streets.

At the bus stop I waited, alone.
  As the cold, cold bus moved,
Silently, towards the station
  I glimpsed the mournful sky,

The littered London streets,
  A lost hungry dog, human bodies
Slumped in the doorways.
  A dazed woman walked aimlessly.

III

Then ... I heard footsteps approaching.
  I turned around —
His eyes were hidden behind
  Old, dark glasses.

As he handed me the ticket I felt
  The icy touch of his emaciated hand.
That early morning in May ...
  My grieving heart was dark as night.

Era una serata fresca d'acqua

E^{ra} Una serata fresca d'acqua

E profumata dalla zagara
E dalle pinete

*

I^{t was} An evening fresh with water

And scented by the orange blossoms
And the pine woods

Dell' amore

D^{ell' amore}

       Conosco

Adesso

      Soltanto

Il Dolore

*

O^{f Love}

     I know

Now

     Only

Sorrow

III
Maria's Chrysanthemums
A Literary Screenplay

Character List

PIETRASANTA MARIA
Maria as a four-year-old girl.
Maria as a newly wed seventeen year old.
Maria as a forty-two-year-old married woman.

GELSOMINO SALVATORE
(In Sicilian dialect Totò)
Totò as a newly wed twenty-five-year-old man.
Totò as a fifty-year-old man.

MARIA'S MOTHER
An elderly woman in her late sixties

MARIA'S CHILDREN
Rosario, aged twenty-three.
Vincenzo, aged fourteen.
Assunta, aged nine.
Anna Maria, aged six.

THE VILLAGE PRIEST
Don Lillo, aged fifty-five.

VINCENZO'S BEST SCHOOL FRIEND
Giuseppe, aged fourteen.

EXTERIOR. SICILIAN HILLSIDE. LATE AFTERNOON.

An almond tree newly blossomed stands on its own on a rocky, breezy hillside in the bright and soft March Sicilian sunlight.

The blossom on the almond tree quivers with the breeze.

Gusts of wind move the blossoms on the branches. A stronger gust blows the petals into the air.

EXTERIOR. LEMON ORCHARD. LATE AFTERNOON.

A lemon orchard on a hillside.

A four year old little girl, MARIA, sways joyfully on a swing suspended from the branches of an old and twisted lemon tree.

Nearby MARIA'S FATHER is hoeing. He is a middle-aged farmer dressed in heavy, olive-green corduroy trousers, with a black velvet waistcoat over a checked shirt. On his head he wears a black cap. His face is unshaven.

His hoeing chafes the soil.

In the background we hear water falling into water as it runs into a nearby trough.

Small birds occasionally fly overhead.

EXTERIOR. LEMON ORCHARD. LATE AFTERNOON.

The infant Maria has a basket full of almond blossoms. She is sitting on a terrace and arranging the blossoms on the ground in the shape of a tree.

As she finishes composing the form of the tree a gust of wind blows the petals away.

Maria begins to cry.

Her father comes to her and picks her up. He rocks her in his arms showing her the floating blossoms.

THIRTEEN YEARS LATER.

INTERIOR. SICILIAN BAROQUE CHURCH. LATE MORNING.

The interior is airy and spare. On both sides two simple rows of columns rise to the roof.

There is a dark red carpet down the aisle. A congregation looks towards a wedding ceremony.

On the altar steps the bride and groom are kneeling on a long red-velvet stool. A PRIEST, in gold ceremonial dress, stands in front of them. Six young girls, aged about four, in white wedding-like dresses and veils over their faces, kneel in a circle around the couple. Each girl holds an orange lily in her hand.

There are also three four-year-old pageboys dressed in dark green velvet suits over crisp white lacey shirts. Around their waists are bands of burgundy silk.

One boy stands on each side of the girls and the third boy stands behind them.

Under her white beaded veil, MARIA aged seventeen, with her dark eyes and long silky black hair, has the melancholy air of a beautiful Sicilian Madonna.

The groom SALVATORE (Totò in Sicilian dialect), aged twenty-five, is a robust, peasant-like figure, with sandy, golden-brown hair.

The congregation is composed of simple country people with a healthy, earthy appearance, dressed in their best festive clothes.

>PRIEST
>*Will you Pietrasanta Maria take Gelsomino Salvatore
>as your lawful wedded husband?*

>MARIA
>*Yes, I will.*

Under her veil momentarily Maria shows a welling up of emotions.

The priest turns to Salvatore.

>PRIEST
>*Will you Gelsomino Salvatore take Pietrasanta Maria
>as your lawful wedded wife?*

>SALVATORE
>*Yes, I will.*

The priest blesses them.

The rich sound of the organ floods the church.

Maria and Salvatore rise. They turn and start walking back down the aisle. She looks out timidly with a contained smile.

One of the bridesmaids lifts the train. The other bridesmaids walk following the couple holding the orange lilies, and they are followed in line by the pageboys.

The immediate relatives and then the guests follow on.

MARIA'S MOTHER, supported by her husband, is red-eyed holding a white handkerchief in her hand and occasionally drying her tears.

EXTERIOR. CHURCH ENTRANCE. LATE MORNING.

A palm tree stands near the entrance of the village church. The wedding party is gathered outside. Old-fashioned cameras held by two photographers start flashing at the couple.

Several young Sicilian girls holding baskets throw white blossoms and handfuls of white rice at the couple.

A few of the younger guests urge the couple to kiss for the camera.

GUESTS
We want you to kiss...
Kiss.. Kiss.

The two photographers bustle into position. Salvatore gently lifts her veil. Maria smiles timidly. Salvatore kisses her.

The guests cheer and applaud.

There are strong contrasts of darkness and light as the branches of the palm tree sway in the morning wind.

EXTERIOR. VILLAGE BELVEDERE. EARLY DUSK.

A mountain village. In the distance, there is a promontory, a huge bay and a dusky calm sea.

Tango music can be faintly heard across the crepuscular landscape. The music gradually swells as a large terrace at the edge of the village slowly comes into full view.

Many people are dancing on the crowded village belvedere.

Tables, arranged in a semi-circle and covered in a white embroidered linen, hold the remains of the wedding banquet. At the centre stands a tall wedding cake with figurines of bride and groom on top. Bottles of sparkling wine, liqueurs and glasses are scattered all over the tables laid with chests of fruits — oranges, apples, bananas, dates ...

Older people are sitting, talking to each other at the sides of the dance area.

A pair of teenage boys stand, resting their arms affectionately over each other's shoulders. Two teenage girls sit talking by the table holding, each other's hands.

Dozens of people are dancing, men dancing with their wives, men dancing with men, children with their parents and grandparents, women with other women.

Totò is standing beside Maria. He glances at her and touches her hand. She looks down shyly as his fingers entwine with hers.

EXTERIOR. TERRACE. DUSK. LATER.

Maria and Totò are dancing together arm-in-arm, surrounded by the circling bridesmaids and pageboys. Two outer circles of friends and relatives are dancing around them.

On the perimeter of the terrace two lines of thick ropes are slung loosely between a number of poles. Sections are covered by twisted branches of citrus trees still bearing their blossoms and small lemon fruits. Wound around the branches are tiny white Christmas-like lights.

The sun is setting over the sea. The bay and the promontory are bathed in the fiery colours of sunset.

The music slowly fades into the background and the darkening landscape recedes.

TWENTY-FIVE YEARS LATER

INTERIOR/EXTERIOR. TERRACE. EARLY MORNING.

MARIA now a woman of forty-two. Pensively she stands looking out over the terrace and the landscape, remembering. Then she turns and walks away.

EXTERIOR. VILLAGE STREET. EARLY MORNING.

Maria has her right arm firmly entwined around her husband's. Totò is fifty. They walk together in silence for a little while. Maria looks at his face and smiles.

TOTÒ
Maria, I shall be a little late tonight.

MARIA
*Will you bring home a bag full of oranges
and some vegetables?*

Totò nods. They walk on.

EXTERIOR. EDGE OF VILLAGE. EARLY MORNING.

Totò stops and they kiss. Totò mounts a mule and
Maria hands him his lunch wrapped in a checked
teatowel.

MARIA
Don't work too late Totò

Maria lingers watching her husband as he rides away for
his day's work.

INTERIOR. BARN. EARLY MORNING.

Maria collects eggs from the straw and puts them into her
apron as chickens and turkeys are running around noisily.

EXTERIOR. BARN.EARLY MORNING.

As Maria leaves the barn, a large flock of sheep passes
by her house. An older shepherd SERAFINO and a younger
shepherd are whistling and waving their crooks
controlling the sheep. Their dogs yap running fast around
the flock.

Maria waits for the flock to pass, holding the eggs in her
apron.

SERAFINO
Good morning. Maria

MARIA
Good morning. Tell Giuseppa
that Totò will come and collect
the ricotta this evening.

INTERIOR/EXTERIOR. KITCHEN. EARLY MORNING.

A rustic stone-flagged kitchen. On a narrow wooden table stand two large bowls, one full of oranges and one of lemons. Glass jars of olives, dried tomatoes and pickled aubergines stand on the shelf.

A framed image of Christ's torso hangs on the wall behind the main kitchen table. Christ holds his bleeding heart in the outstretched palms of his hands. On his head rests a crown of thorns. Beads of blood trickle down his temples.

On the main table there is a vase full of wild flowers. From the ceiling clusters of cherry tomatoes hang like chandeliers amongst bunches of herbs, oregano and thyme.

Maria lays her apron on the kitchen table. Unfolding it she takes the eggs and places them on a plate.

On the window sill there are pots of basil, mint and rosemary. She looks out to the hillside.

The flock of sheep is shepherded towards the countryside. The shepherds whistle and wave their rough sticks as the dogs bark and run around in all directions.

EXTERIOR. PATH. EARLY MORNING.

Totò rides his mule along stony and uneven country tracks. The fields and banks on each side of the tracks are covered with wild spring flowers. The hooves of the mule clack on the stony ground. The mountains and the sea are infused with the colours of an early dawn.

INTERIOR. KITCHEN. EARLY MORNING.

Maria is still gazing out over the terrace and across to the hills.

EXTERIOR. ROCKY COUNTRYSIDE. EARLY MORNING.

The sheep are further in the distance. Like a flowing stream they wind their way over the rugged landscape.

INTERIOR. KITCHEN. MORNING. LATER.

Maria is humming as she prepares breakfast. Milk and a coffee pot are on the stove. Maria counts four eggs into a pot of boiling water.

On the table, there is a tin full of Sicilian biscuits and around it there are four milk bowls.

INTERIOR. KITCHEN. MORNING. LATER.

At the table sit her three children, ANNA MARIA aged six, ASSUNTA aged nine, and VINCENZO aged fourteen. They are dunking their biscuits in their milk bowls. They tease and joke with each other.

MARIA
Vincenzo, have you put your homework in your bag?

VINCENZO
Oh no, it's upstairs.

Vincenzo runs out to collect it.

Assunta is eating languidly.

ASSUNTA
Mamma, Mamma, I feel sick.

MARIA
What's the matter Assunta?

ASSUNTA
I don't know, Mamma, I don't know.

Maria places her hand on Assunta's forehead.

MARIA
Don't worry, you're only tired.
You have been up too late.

Maria pats her on the head. Assunta smiles.

MARIA
You will feel better later.

Maria kisses her.

EXTERIOR. CENTRE OF VILLAGE. EARLY MORNING.

Assunta and Anna Maria are dressed in their school
clothes, black aprons with red ribbons around their
collars. Maria holds Anna Maria by the hand as she tugs
on her mother's skirt. Vincenzo and Assunta follow.

EXTERIOR. SCHOOL ENTRANCE. EARLY MORNING.

In the bustling school entrance, Maria watches her children run off and join the others.

Maria talks with some of the other women.

EXTERIOR. CHURCH. MORNING.

A simple, white fronted, village church.

INTERIOR. CHURCH. MORNING.

A few parishioners are sitting whilst a church service is taking place. DON LILLO aged fifty-five, the village priest, plump-faced and cheery is celebrating Mass.

EXTERIOR. TOTÒ'S LAND. LATE MORNING.

Totò, unshaven, is hoeing. He is wearing his black cap, olive green corduroy trousers, checked shirt, dark red cord waistcoat and neckchief.

He is watering vegetables.

Totò is picking oranges and lemons and putting them in baskets.

Totò clears the weeds. He wipes his brow.

Totò sits under an old carob tree eating his lunch.

Totò has a siesta under the shade of the carob tree with his black cap tilted down over his eyes. Two dogs lie near him under the tree. The mule is restless in the shadows as insects buzz around his ears.

In the distance there are fields of olive trees with their silver leaves swaying in the wind. Slopes are covered with almond trees in blossom moving in the breeze.

EXTERIOR. MARIA'S COURTYARD. LATE MORNING.

Maria has her hair in plaits held by pins and tied in a knot behind the nape of her neck.

She unties the plaits and loosens her hair. She bends and lets her hair fall and places her head under the running water. The water runs off her hair into a bucket below.

She washes and soaps her hair.

EXTERIOR. HOUSE TERRACE. LATE MORNING.

Maria sits humming in the morning sunshine, combing out her hair and letting the sun dry it.

She is contented.

She notices a male neighbour watching her. She turns away from him.

EXTERIOR. HOUSE COURTYARD. LATE MORNING.

Maria is working outside in the courtyard. She cuts, salts and lays cut tomatoes on wooden boards. She tastes the fruit.

She carries the wooden boards and places them on the terrace wall in the sunshine.

Pots of basil, rosemary, carnations and geraniums are placed around the terrace. Bunches of cherry tomatoes hang against the walls, together with herbs and bunches of dried garlic.

There is a hutch with a few rabbits inside. Chickens and turkeys roam around.

EXTERIOR. SCHOOL. AFTERNOON.

Maria waits at the school gates. A bell rings and children come running. Assunta and Anna Maria are in their midst.

EXTERIOR. TOTÒ'S PLOT. EARLY DUSK.

Totò is getting ready to go home. Under the carob tree there are small piles of oranges, lemons, carrots and wild vegetables. He fills the linen saddlebag with his goods. He carries the saddlebag and hangs it over the back of the mule. Leaves of the vegetables protrude from the bag.

Totò cuts wild roses from the edge of a field. He places the wild roses with the vegetables.

EXTERIOR. COUNTRY PATH. EARLY DUSK.

In greased boots Totò walks, dusty in appearance pulling his mule along by its rein.

EXTERIOR. VILLAGE. EARLY MORNING.

The village lies perched between two hills.

EXTERIOR. VILLAGE MARKET. MORNING.

A small market. Villagers are laying out fruit and vegetables to sell.

EXTERIOR. VILLAGE CORSO (MAIN.STREET) AFTERNOON.

Groups of unshaven men are sitting in front of their *circoli* (social clubs) smoking and talking.

EXTERIOR. EDGE OF VILLAGE. EARLY DUSK.

From the edge of the village, Maria with Assunta and Anna Maria walk towards Totò.

Totò is riding the mule, with the saddlebags full of fruit and vegetables. Long leaves of artichokes and soft twigs covered with orange blossoms protrude from the bag.

EXTERIOR. EDGE OF VILLAGE. EARLY DUSK.

As Totò gets closer he dismounts from the mule. Anna Maria runs to him.

> ANNA MARIA
> *Papa, papa.*

Totò picks up Anna Maria and puts her on the mule. When Totò meets Maria he kisses her on the cheek.

They hold hands as Assunta leads the mule. Together they walk towards their house.

INTERIOR. HOUSE. KITCHEN. EVENING.

Maria is preparing supper. Totò is playing with the children. There is a knock at the door. Totò goes to open the door.

Don Lillo enters carrying a couple of bottles of home-made wine. Totò speaks obsequiously.

TOTÒ
Don Lillo, Don Lillo, good evening.
Come in. Come in.

DON LILLO
Totò, good evening. Maria, good evening.

Maria moves to greet Don Lillo smiling.

MARIA
Nice to see you Don Lillo.
Make yourself at home.

Assunta and Anna Maria run to him. Don Lillo strokes
Assunta's head. Maria offers Don Lillo a chair near the
stove.

Anna Maria jumps on his knees. Don Lillo bounces her
up and down affectionately. Vincenzo is stoking the fire.

Totò pulls out a chair places it close to Don Lillo and sits.

DON LILLO
How's work? Have you enough water for the summer?

TOTÒ
I am having another well dug for the vegetables.
The oranges and lemons
drain far too much water.

DON LILLO
I have decided to buy a small tractor for my wheatfield.

The children exchange glances..

ANNA MARIA
A tractor.

DON LILLO
The work is getting too hard for me.

ANNA MARIA
Will you take me for a ride on the tractor?

DON LILLO
Yes, of course.

DON LILLO
And you Vincenzo
how are you getting on at school?

VINCENZO
I find the mathematics very hard.

DON LILLO
Never mind. You must persevere
in order to pass your exams.

Maria places a bowl of steaming hot minestrone on the table.

MARIA
Everyone take a seat.

INTERIOR. KITCHEN. EVENING.

The family and Don Lillo are eating. On a side table, there is a vase full of wild roses.

TOTÒ
To get my land to produce requires
long hours. It is so much work.

MARIA
We should thank God that we have our health.

TOTÒ
When I go to the market to sell my
produce, people only want to pay very little.

DON LILLO
The land may be hard, Totò, but look
around your table, you cannot say that you
are not a fortunate man...
Have you heard Totò
the council is applying to the Reggione
for money to asphalt the road out towards your land?

Anna Maria stares at the pasta not wanting to eat.

TOTÒ
That will make my journey easier...
Come on Anna Maria, eat your pasta.

MARIA
It will make you grow.

ANNA MARIA
But I'm not hungry.

MARIA
If you want to become as
tall as your sister,
you must eat your pastà.

Anna Maria pulls a face and fiddles with her spoon on
her plate.

TOTÒ
Your mother is right,
if you don't eat you
will get smaller and smaller.

Anna Maria becomes radiant and begins eating.

INTERIOR. KITCHEN. EVENING.

The kitchen table is clear. Totò is smoking and playing cards with Don Lillo.

Maria is sitting by the stove knitting a pullover. The fire crackles.

DON LILLO
How is your son Rosario doing?
Has he found a job in Milan?

MARIA
My brother found him a job in the bar
where he works. He seems happy there.

Maria glances at Totò.

TOTÒ
He just didn't want to work on the land.

Totò for a moment looks sad. Maria looks towards the fire.

EXTERIOR. VILLAGE. DAWN.

The break of dawn. The first glimmers of the rising sun appear on the sea's horizon.

The mountains are still in semi-darkness. The immense sea is quiescent.

The countryside is slowly awakening with soft and varied colours.

The village streets are empty. Dogs bark in the stillness of an early dawn.

The main street becomes silent again.

Cockerels crow.

The shops and houses are shuttered. At one end of the street stands the church. Church bells begin resounding in the early morning stillness.

INTERIOR. MARIA'S BEDROOM. DAWN

Maria awakes and gently shakes Totò on the shoulder. Totò stirs.

EXTERIOR. MAIN STREET. DAWN.

The main street is again silent and empty. There comes the tinkling of tiny bells.

EXTERIOR. MAIN STREET. DAWN.

The street is filled with sheep and goats. Bells ring from their necks. Shepherds and young boys are shouting and whistling. Dogs are barking.

EXTERIOR. MARIA'S HOUSE. DAWN.

Outside Maria's house there is a farmer with a cow. Maria hands him an aluminium bowl, which the farmer places under the cow's udder. The farmer squeezes the milk from the cow and the milk rings against the aluminium bowl. As it fills the bowl it froths.

EXTERIOR. MAIN SQUARE. DAWN.

A row of labourers wait, chatting and smoking, dressed in rustic corduroy clothes, ready for work. Some lean back against a railing. They hold their lunches wrapped in tea-towels.

EXTERIOR. STREET. DAWN.

The sheep are winding down narrow streets.

EXTERIOR. EDGE OF VILLAGE. DAWN.

In the distance the flock spills out into the countryside.

EXTERIOR. VILLAGE. DAWN.

Maria and Totò walk side by side to the edge of the village.

They stop. Maria hands Totò his lunch.
Totò leads the mule away with the rein.

As Totò leaves the village behind Maria watches him descend the stony pathways until he disappears into the landscape.

INTERIOR. CHURCH. MID-MORNING.

A simple village church. Maria is arranging flowers on the altar with three other village women of different ages, one of whom is in mourning and wears black.

Another woman talks to Maria as she moves the flowers gently.

WOMAN
I love these flowers
Once, I remember a young man
gave me a huge bunch..

A middle-aged church organist arrives greeting the women. They return his greeting. He disappears behind the organ.

The women continue with the floral decorations. The little church fills with the sound of the organ as the organist starts practising.

EXTERIOR. MAIN STREET. MORNING.

Death bells toll in the village. A funeral procession leaves the church passing into the main street. The procession is headed by a row of men carrying large garlands of flowers followed by Don Lillo doing his best to look sombre. Several altar boys are scattering incense as they walk. The coffin is carried by mourners followed by a cluster of grieving women in black. Behind them there are many villagers. Maria, alone, follows a few paces apart at the end of the procession.

EXTERIOR. COUNTRYSIDE. MORNING.

Vincenzo and another boy of fourteen, GIUSEPPE, are walking side by side.

VINCENZO
Shall we go climbing?

GIUSEPPE
No, swimming?

VINCENZO
I know where..

Vincenzo starts to run.

EXTERIOR. COUNTRYSIDE. MORNING.

Vincenzo and Giuseppe run playing through the countryside.

They run through tall wheatfields of gold.

They walk through orange groves, the branches heavy with fruits.

EXTERIOR. ORANGE GROVE. AFTERNOON

They two boys reach a cement cistern full of water.

The branches of the orange trees, weighed down with fruit, can be seen reflected in the water.

The boys undress themselves excitedly. They climb onto the edge of the basin and plunge into the water. As they play, splashing around, the water overflows.

EXTERIOR. ORANGE GROVE CISTERN. AFTERNOON

Vincenzo climbs out of the basin dripping with water.

He lies in the sun face down on the grass. Giuseppe comes and lies next to him.

INTERIOR. BAR. EVENING.

Totò is in a smoke-filled room playing cards with other men. The room is full of men of different ages, many unshaven, some wearing black caps, talking, smoking, drinking, laughing. Behind the counter the bar owner chats with customers expansively.

EXTERIOR. MARIA'S HOUSE. NIGHT.

Totò comes in and puts down his cap on the table. He rests in a chair. Maria goes to him and puts her hand affectionately over his shoulders.

INTERIOR. MARIA'S BEDROOM. NIGHT.

In semi-darkness Maria and Totò, naked on their bed, are making love.

EXTERIOR. FIELD. MORNING.

Assunta and Anna Maria are playing on the swing hanging from the branches of a carob tree.

Totò sits watching them. Sicilian music plays from a radio.

EXTERIOR. MARIA'S HOUSE TERRACE. MORNING.

Music is playing.

Maria is putting a sun-dried tomato paste with basil and garlic into glass jars. She pours olive oil into the jars. Several jars are full.

Anna Maria is playing with a ball bouncing it on the terrace. It knocks a pot of basil which falls and breaks open on the ground.

MARIA
Anna Maria! I told you not to play here with the ball.

Anna Maria starts crying. Maria wipes her hands with a tea towel and picks up Anna Maria and kisses her.

MARIA
You mustn't cry, never mind.

EXTERIOR. MARIA'S HOUSE TERRACE. LATER.

Anna Maria stands on a chair next to Maria and another woman at a table filling sun-dried tomatoes. Plates of sliced garlic, oregano and basil leaves are spread across the table.

In one corner of the terrace MARIA'S MOTHER dressed completely in black sits silently watching them. Her face is furrowed with age.

Anna Maria puts her hand into a jar of sun-dried tomatoes and surreptitiously eats some. Maria's mother is annoyed and indicates this to Maria. Maria sees Anna Maria and smiles.

INTERIOR. MARIA'S HOUSE MAY. MORNING.

It's Assunta's first communion. She stands in a white, wedding-like dress. Maria places a veil over her head. Assunta looks at herself in a mirror. She looks like a young bride.

ASSUNTA
Mamma, this dress suits me so well.

MARIA
You look beautiful.

On the table there is a vase full of orange lilies. Maria takes a lily, dries the stem with a kitchen cloth and hands it to Assunta.

Maria stands back from Assunta. She calls Totò and together they look at her with pride exchanging an affectionate glance with each other.

INTERIOR. CHURCH. LATE AFTERNOON.

Parents dressed in their best clothes sit in the pews watching on.

Assunta and a row of girls of her age dressed in white kneel in front of the altar.

Don Lillo is celebrating Mass.

Totò glances at Maria, who is watching the ceremony intently.

EXTERIOR. HILLSIDE DREAM. EARLY DUSK.

A breeze blows. A long line of young girls dressed in white bride-like clothes, with veils over their heads, each holding an orange lily, walk as in a dream along the ridge of a hill.

A priest in embroidered gold leads the young girls with three altar boys swinging thuribles of smoking incense in the air behind them.

The procession moves along the breezy ridge which is smothered with wild flowers. The girls's veils are blown by the breeze.

EXTERIOR. OUTDOOR TERRACE. DUSK.

Many guests are gathered on the terrace for the first communion party.

Tables covered with crisp white linen hold the remains of the feast, bowls of fruit, cakes and sweets.

Assunta is dancing to Latin music, with other girls and boys.

EXTERIOR. OUTDOOR TERRACE. LATER

Maria looks on happily with Totò.

Men dance with men, women with women, men with women, grandparents with children, boys with boys, girls with girls.

Totò takes Assunta's hand and they begin dancing together.

On the edge of the dancing area Vincenzo sits beside Giuseppe who stands with his arm over Vincenzo's shoulders.

EXTERIOR. OUTDOOR TERRACE. EVENING.

The party has become bigger. The terrace is now full of people, neighbours and villagers, dancing and drinking.

Maria and Totò dance happily together arm in arm.

Other girls dressed in first communion white have also joined the party. They dance in a circle. Boys form an outer circle around them.

We see the dusky mountains and the pearly sea and the fiery colours of a late sunset. Latin music slowly fades out.

EXTERIOR. MOUNTAINS. EARLY MORNING.

A blue bus twists its way down the narrow mountain road with the blue sea in the distance.

INTERIOR. BUS. EARLY MORNING.

The bus is full of farmers. Hard-wearing linen bags and baskets full of country produce rest on the seats and floor. Totò talks to another farmer. The bus draws to a stop in the middle of the countryside. An elderly peasant woman wearing a black headscarf and her husband wearing a cap get off.

INTERIOR. EXTERIOR. BUS. MOUNTAINS. EARLY MORNING.

Totò is looking out of the window. In the distance close to the sea, Cefalù's massive cathedral is jutting up into the sky.

EXTERIOR. HARBOUR. EARLY MORNING.

The bus stops at the harbour. Totò and the other farmers get out of the bus carrying their bags of produce with them.

EXTERIOR. PROMENADE. EARLY MORNING.

With the other farmers Totò walks along the promenade carrying his bags and baskets of fruit and vegetables.

EXTERIOR. MARKET. EARLY MORNING.

The bustle of the market. Stalls are laid out. Traders are shouting; townspeople are buying.

EXTERIOR. TERRACE. EARLY MORNING.

Maria carries a basket of wet clothes. She puts the basket on the floor and takes a container full of wooden pegs from the corner of the terrace floor. She sings as she takes out a laced sheet and hangs it on the washing line with the pegs.

EXTERIOR. MARKET. LATER.

Totò has displayed all his goods on his stall. There are baskets of lemons, artichokes and wild vegetables. Totò looks out across the market and sees many stalls laid out.

EXTERIOR. MARKET. LATER.

Totò is selling some vegetables to a customer, who puts them into a bag.

EXTERIOR. VILLAGE. MORNING.

Maria walks along a passage. An old woman sits in a doorway. Maria stops to talk to her for a moment.

Then she leaves with the slightest of waves.

EXTERIOR. VILLAGE STREET. MORNING.

Maria meets and stops to talk to a woman of her own age in the street.

EXTERIOR. BAKERY. MORNING.

Maria walks towards the village bakery and enters.

INTERIOR. BAKERY. MORNING.

The bakery is crowded. Maria is greeted warmly by the baker. Maria purchases some bread. She exchanges some words with the other customers.

EXTERIOR. MARKET. AFTERNOON.

Totò has sold his produce and is packing up his things. He counts the little money that he has taken.

EXTERIOR. SCHOOL. AFTERNOON

Maria waits in front of the school chatting with other parents at the gates.

Moments later the children pour out of the building noisily.

Assunta and Anna Maria run towards her. She kisses them and takes them by the hand.

EXTERIOR. COURTYARD. AFTERNOON

Totò has a siesta under the shadow of a tree. His black cap is pulled down over his face.

Maria ushers in the children who are singing and joking with each other. They stop when they see their father asleep. Totò flips up his cap to look.

TOTÒ
Ah, you're here.

EXTERIOR. MOUNTAIN ROAD. EVENING.

Vincenzo is riding on a Vespa with Giuseppe down winding mountains paths.

INTERIOR. MARIA'S HOUSE. EVENING.

Assunta and Anna Maria are sitting side by side. Assunta is helping Anna Maria to read. She moves her finger along the words in a book.

Assunta and Anna Maria read the words of the text together.

ASSUNTA AND ANNA MARIA
In the springtime the wild flowers
bloom and the almond trees blossom..

EXTERIOR. SEA. ROCKS. EVENING.

Vincenzo and Giuseppe are standing on the rocks with four other boys, all wearing thin costumes. The boys dive one by one into the sea. Giuseppe dives second last and then finally Vincenzo dives.

INTERIOR. KITCHEN. EVENING.

Totò, Maria, Vincenzo, Assunta and Anna Maria are eating. A television is on in the background.

INTERIOR. OVEN ROOM. NIGHT.

Maria in a black headscarf is feeding the fire with wood. The wood is burning fiercely. She takes a trowel full of almond shells and tips them into the fire. The fire crackles as the shells ignite.

INTERIOR. OVEN ROOM. NIGHT.

Near the oven there are wooden boards covered with white linen cloths.

Maria takes off the white linen cloth, underneath which there is a large roll of dough.

INTERIOR. OVEN ROOM. NIGHT.

Maria throws flour on a wooden base. Then she flattens the dough. Several pizzas are already made. Maria lays tomatoes and marinated artichokes on the pizza base.

INTERIOR. OVEN ROOM. NIGHT.

Maria pushes metal platters laid with the dough into the oven. Totò, unnoticed, watches her for a moment.

She takes out hot cooked pies from the oven and puts them on the table. She cuts one which is full of steaming spinach.

On a table there is a cooked turkey with almonds and rosemary.

TOTÒ
Maria.

INTERIOR. BEDROOM. NIGHT.

Totò lies asleep in bed. Maria looks tenderly towards him, crosses herself and puts out the light.

EXTERIOR. CHURCH. DAY.

Don Lillo leaves the church, closing the church door. He walks along the Corso (main street). Groups of elderly men sit outside smoking and talking.

The men greet Don Lillo as he passes. Don Lillo acknowledges them, nodding.

EXTERIOR. MAIN STREET. EVENING.

Totò and Don Lillo stroll up and down the main Corso.

DON LILLO
They have now finished the road, Totò.

TOTÒ
I've decided to buy a Vespa.
My journey to work will be made so much easier.

DON LILLO
How will you pay?

TOTÒ
I will pay by monthly installments.

INTERIOR. MARIA'S HOUSE. EVENING.

Don Lillo and Totò enter. Don Lillo hands Maria two bottles of wine which he has made himself.

The table is already laid.

MARIA
Thank you for the wine, Don Lillo,
but you shouldn't have gone to the trouble.

DON LILLO
Oh, it's nothing, it's nothing.

INTERIOR. KITCHEN. EVENING.

Maria's family and Don Lillo are sitting around the table eating. Anna Maria sits to one side of Don Lillo, Vincenzo to the other.

On a narrow table by the wall are laid spinach pies, pizzas, bread and a roast turkey.

ANNA MARIA
Don Lillo, I can read now.

DON LILLO
Excellent. Will you read something to me?

Anna Maria gets up and runs out.

DON LILLO
How is the digging of your well going?

TOTÒ
They have come across a rock, so
they have to start digging in another place.

Anna Maria returns to Don Lillo with her book. She climbs on his knees and opens the book. She begins reading, tracing the words with her finger.

> ANNA MARIA
> *In springtime the wild flowers bloom*
> *and the almond trees blossom*

Anna Maria hesitates on the word blossom.
Maria whispers.

> ANNA MARIA
> *..blossom*
> *and the birds move restlessly*
> *over the trees.*

> DON LILLO
> *Bravo, Bravo!*

Anna Maria puts the book down satisfied.

INTERIOR. KITCHEN. EVENING. LATER.

Anna Maria and Assunta have gone to bed. Totò, Maria and Vincenzo sit by the stove with Don Lillo.

> DON LILLO
> *When you finish school will you work*
> *with your father in the country?*

> MARIA
> *First he has to study very hard to pass his exams.*

VINCENZO
After I have passed my exams I want to go
to Milan and visit my brother and my uncle
and spend the summer months working there.

DON LILLO
Then what do you want to do?

VINCENZO
I want to do the concorso
and enter the Guardia di Finanza.

DON LILLO
I see.

VINCENZO
I like the city and I want
a secure job and I can wear a uniform.

TOTÒ
(To Don Lillo)
Working the land is hard and there is no money in it.
Young men of today want life to be easy.

DON LILLO
Oh, they are too easily seduced
by what they see on television.

MARIA
They will all be leaving us soon.

EXTERIOR. MARIA'S HOUSE. DAWN.

Totò opens the barn door. Maria stands by watching Totò admiringly take out a new Vespa.

He hangs a linen bag over the saddle of the Vespa. Then he mounts the Vespa and rides off.

EXTERIOR. ASPHALT. ROAD. DAWN.

Totò rides the Vespa along a twisting mountain road.

EXTERIOR. ANOTHER ROAD. DAWN.

Totò rides the Vespa along a newly asphalted road. He turns off the new road onto a stony track.

He overtakes a farmer with his donkey.

EXTERIOR. STONY TRACK. DAWN.

Totò rides the Vespa along a bumpy stony track.

EXTERIOR. PLOT OF LAND. DAWN.

Totò is working, watering vegetables.

The Vespa, covered with a blanket, is in the shade of a fig tree.

EXTERIOR. PLOT OF LAND. MORNING.

Totò is digging the land.

EXTERIOR. PLOT OF LAND. MID DAY

Totò is sitting on the ground under the shadow of a carob tree. He eats his lunch from a small plastic box which contains peppered cheese, a piece of bread, olives and a tomato.

EXTERIOR. PLOT OF LAND. LATER.

A neighbouring older farmer arrives. Totò rises and greets him. The farmer sits with Totò under the tree. Totò pours red wine into two cups and he offers him the wine. They drink and talk together.

OLD FARMER
Now that I'm getting older
I need someone to help me.
My son doesn't want to study and
he doesn't want to learn how to
work the land either.
I don't know what to do with him.

TOTÒ
Yes, when I get older I will also have no-one.

EXTERIOR. HOUSE. EVENING. LATER.

Totò pulls up on the Vespa and unloads some produce.

EXTERIOR. TERRACE. EVENING.

Maria and Assunta are swinging a rope. Anna Maria is skipping. Totò approaches, watching amused.

EXTERIOR. TERRACE. EVENING.

Totò is sitting on the balustrade watching Maria.

At a table Maria is preparing bunches of basil, oregano and cherry tomatoes to hang.

Totò gets up and moves across to Maria tenderly and with a gesture of affection takes a bunch of basil from her hands and places it on the table. He takes her hands and holds them together, almost as if in prayer. They look into each other's eyes with an inner recognition.

EXTERIOR. SEASCAPE. DAWN.

Dawn breaks on the silvered sea.

EXTERIOR. WELL. MORNING.

Totò is drawing water from a well.

EXTERIOR. PLOT OF LAND. AFTERNOON

Totò carefully pours water from a bucket into the furrows of the earth along the lines of artichokes.

EXTERIOR. PLOT OF LAND. EARLY DUSK.

Little piles of blood oranges, lemons, artichokes and wild vegetables are resting stacked on the ground.

Totò places fruit and vegetables in the linen bag, filling it.

Baskets and bags of fruits and vegetables stand ready on the ground.

Totò lifts a full bag brimming with artichokes and lays it over the seat of the Vespa.

Then he puts a second bag full of blood oranges over his shoulder and climbs onto the bike.

EXTERIOR. STONY PATH. EARLY DUSK.

Totò rides the Vespa along a stony track. He overtakes a farmer who is riding home on his mule. They exchange a greeting.

EXTERIOR. STONY TRACK. EARLY DUSK.

A rugged stone is in the middle of the of the track.

EXTERIOR. STONY TRACK. EARLY DUSK.

Totò rides along the bumpy track. In front of him the track is rutted and dry.

EXTERIOR. STONY TRACK. EARLY DUSK

Totò approaches a bend in the road and rounds the bend out of sight.

EXTERIOR. STONY TRACK. EARLY DUSK.

Totò's black cap lies on the ground. The Vespa is overturned, its wheels spinning fast.

Totò is lying on the ground.

The blood oranges roll out of the bag onto the track; some roll into the ditch, others are fractured and bleeding on the ground.

Totò lifts himself up effortlessly.

He picks up the spilled oranges one by one, leaving the fractured ones on the ground.

He touches his temple.

On the palm of his right hand he notices some traces of dark red blood, shining under the sun's light.

His gaze then turns towards the stone. It too is stained with the same velvety blood.

At that very moment and before he realises the gravity of what has happened, Totò loses consciousness.

His body falls once again onto the stony and uneven track.

The little blood oranges come rolling out of the linen bag for a second time.

Some rest around his head; others, a few of which on impact have begun bleeding, roll away into the ditch.

A trickling stream of blood reaches Totò's unshaven chin.

His eyes are gently closed.

His black cap lies close to his head revealing his sandy brown hair.

His thick corduroy trousers are torn at the knee.

The sun begins to lose its strength while the surrounding countryside begins to relish the cooling glow of sunset.

His body remains motionless.

EXTERIOR. STONY TRACK. DUSK. LATER.

The farmer on his mule comes within sight of Totò.

EXTERIOR. STONY TRACK. DUSK. MOMENTS LATER.

The farmer is bending over Totò.

Totò is breathing shallowly.

The oranges surround his head.

In a state of agitation, the farmer shakes Totò.

FARMER
Totò! Totò! Totò!
Can you hear me?
Can you hear me?

EXTERIOR. VILLAGE. DUSK. LATER.

In the distance the village is immersed in the now advanced and lingering shades of dusk.

INTERIOR. BARE ROOM. DAY

A bare and semi-darkened large room holds the weeping and laments of women.

Slanting light from a venetian blind filters across the ceiling and the corners of the bare walls.

Patterns of light flicker on the floor.

The room is grey and cold.

In the centre of the room a line of black shoes and stockinged feet form a crescent.

A semi-circle of women, lamenting and weeping, sit on peasant wicker chairs, all dressed in black and covered in shawls.

Maria is in the middle of the women. She is silent, rocking in grief.

EXTERIOR. MARIA'S HOUSE. DAWN.

Outside, pinned on the door, there is a strip of black edged paper. The words on the paper read:

IN MOURNING
FOR MY
BELOVED HUSBAND

Black drapery hangs over and surrounds the door.

INTERIOR. MARIA'S HOUSE. DAY

Maria's relatives and neighbours cluster around her consoling her. Maria remains stoic and unmoved.

Vincenzo gently touches her arm. Maria places her hand on his.

INTERIOR. MARIA'S HOUSE. DAY.

Maria is sitting glumly on a chair within the frame of an internal door.

Anna Maria looks at her miserably, not knowing what to say.

Maria looks up to Anna Maria blankly.

INTERIOR. BEDROOM. DAY.

Maria is on her bed in semi-darkness. Over the bed is a photograph of Totò framed by a rosary. A votive light flickers under the photograph.

The room is bare. A picture of the Madonna Addolorata covered in a black mantle hangs on another wall.

EXTERIOR. HOUSE. DAWN.

Maria goes out of the house covered in a black shawl. She carries a small spray of wild roses which she holds to her breast.

EXTERIOR. COBBLED VILLAGE STREET. DAWN.

Maria's footsteps resound in the emptiness of the village streets.

EXTERIOR. VILLAGE STREET. DAWN.

Maria walks with her head held down covered by her shawl.

EXTERIOR. VILLAGE STEPS. DAWN.

Maria climbs the steps sullenly.

EXTERIOR. VILLAGE. DAWN.

The diminishing figure of Maria moves through the bare and empty village streets.

EXTERIOR. EDGE OF VILLAGE. DAWN.

Maria leaves the village behind and walks out onto the main road.

A solitary car suddenly speeds past her.

EXTERIOR. CEMETERY. LATE DAWN.

Maria, self absorbed, walks though the gates of the cemetery.

EXTERIOR. CEMETERY. AVENUE. LATE DAWN.

Maria walks along the cypress-lined avenue of the cemetery.

EXTERIOR. CEMETERY. GRAVE. LATE DAWN.

Maria kneels by the headstone. She kisses the studio photograph of young Totò, taken at the time of their marriage.

She takes a vase.

EXTERIOR. CEMETERY TAP. DAWN.

Water gushes from a large tap onto the ground. Maria places the vase under the tap and it quickly overflows with water.

EXTERIOR. CEMETERY GRAVE. LATE DAWN.

She places the wild roses in the water-filled vase and places it underneath her husband's framed photograph.

INTERIOR. KITCHEN. EVENING.

Assunta, Anna Maria and Vincenzo are sitting silently, eating.

They exchange glances silently, without knowing what to say.

INTERIOR. OVEN ROOM. NIGHT.

Maria starts a fire in the oven with twigs and straw which start to burn and crackle.

INTERIOR. BEDROOM. NIGHT.

Maria takes all her coloured clothes from cupboards and drawers.

INTERIOR. KITCHEN. NIGHT.

Maria feeds her clothing into the burning fire of the oven. Her face reflects the red glow of the fire.

EXTERIOR. TERRACE. DAWN.

Maria stands on the balcony looking out into the distance at the hazy boundary between sea and sky.

EXTERIOR. VILLAGE STREET. MORNING.

A busy noisy street.

Maria, dressed all in black, holds Assunta and Anna Maria by the hands as she takes them to school.

She approaches the old woman sitting in her doorway. The old woman greets her. Maria doesn't respond and she continues walking.

Anna Maria turns back smiling to the old woman and breaks contact with her mother's hand.

Maria walks on regardless.

Anna Maria hesitates then runs back after Maria.

INTERIOR. CHURCH. DAY

Maria in black is sitting at the back of the church, all alone.

Don Lillo sees her and walks towards her. She rises and leaves the church.

Don Lillo pauses and watches her leave.

EXTERIOR. CEMETERY GRAVE. DAWN.

Maria is sitting alone by Totò's black marbled grave.

EXTERIOR. MARIA'S HOUSE. EVENING.

The drapery (fading, dusty and slightly tattered) still adorns Maria's front door. Don Lillo stands worriedly casting his eyes over it.

INTERIOR. MARIA'S HOUSE. EVENING.

Maria hears a knock at the door. She hesitates, then she walks to the door but does not immediately open it.

She finally opens the door. Don Lillo pauses on the threshold.

Assunta and Anna Maria look on.

> MARIA
> *Come in.*

Don Lillo enters the room and walks to Anna Maria and Assunta and pats them on the shoulders.

Maria makes a sign for the children to leave the room. Reluctantly they leave.

> INTERIOR . MARIA'S HOUSE. EVENING. LATER.

Don Lillo stands by Maria, speaking gently to her as she prepares vegetables.

> DON LILLO
> *Maria, two months have passed
> now and you have not removed
> the drapery from your door.*

> MARIA
> *Is it really two months?.*

> DON LILLO
> *It is long enough.*

There is a heavy silence.

> DON LILLO
> *I understand that
> you are not greeting people
> in the streets?*

MARIA
Really?

DON LILLO
*The people in the village are not used
to seeing you like this.*

MARIA
(closing her eyes and sighing under her breath)
It is darkness.

DON LILLO
*Maria, I know the depth of
your suffering...*

Maria stoically and slightly nervous continues washing vegetables.

DON LILLO
We were all devoted to Totò.

Anna Maria, listlessly resting her shoulder on the doorframe, hesitates then comes in.

MARIA
Go to your sister! Get ready for bed!

ANNA MARIA
(nervously)
But I'm not sleepy yet.

MARIA
We are busy

Anna Maria reluctantly turns away.

DON LILLO
I know that you visit
the cemetery each break of dawn.

MARIA
Is this what the neighbours are telling you?

Maria walks nervously towards the window.

DON LILLO
Totò was a good soul.
I am sure that he would not want to
see you in this state.

MARIA
Don Lillo...no one can possibly
understand what I feel.
Not even I...
Only after he'd gone did I realise
how much I loved him...
My suffering now is as great
as was my love for him.

Don Lillo looks at her with dismay. Maria offers Don Lillo some glimmer of hope.

MARIA
Don Lillo, tomorrow I'll come to the church
to arrange the flowers.

DON LILLO
Good.

Anna Maria pushes the door open again and stands, with her shoulders resting against the doorframe, looking through into the room.

Don Lillo smiles at her. Maria accompanies Don Lillo to the door.

> MARIA
> (to Anna Maria)
> *You can come in now.*

Don Lillo pauses by the door.

> DON LILLO
> *And I will see you tomorrow at Mass?*

> MARIA
> *Yes.*

Don Lillo nods.

EXTERIOR. CEMETERY. DAWN.

Maria places flowers on Totò's black grave.

EXTERIOR. CHURCH. MORNING.

Don Lillo stands outside the church watching as the congregation leaves.

INTERIOR. CHURCH. DAY.

Maria is alone in the church arranging the flowers. Don Lillo enters and walks towards her. His footsteps resound in the emptiness of the church. Don Lillo comes beside her.

> DON LILLO
> *Maria*

Maria nods.

She continues arranging the flowers not looking towards him.

> DON LILLO
> *You have always arranged flowers*
> *with Carmela and Rosaria.*

> MARIA
> *I like to be on my own at the moment.*

> DON LILLO
> *You need company. It is good*
> *for you to be with other people.*

Maria nervously moves the flowers.

Don Lillo rests his right hand on her shoulder.

> DON LILLO
> *You must have courage.*

Maria, in a state of contained despair and feeling heavily the weight of his hand, abruptly moves away.
Don Lillo's hand falls.

> DON LILLO
> *This morning. you weren't at Mass?*

> MARIA
> *No I wasn't.*

Don Lillo looks away despairingly.

EXTERIOR. CHURCH. AFTERNOON

Maria walks out of the church in a black shawl.

EXTERIOR. EDGE OF VILLAGE. AFTERNOON

Maria leaves the village behind.

EXTERIOR. ROAD. AFTERNOON.

Maria picks some wild flowers by the roadside then she walks off the road.

EXTERIOR. FIELD OF FLOWERS. AFTERNOON.

Maria walks through a field smothered in wild flowers.

She stops here and there picking flowers and adds them to the little bunch which she already holds.

EXTERIOR. ROCKY MOORLAND. DUSK.

Maria roams amongst the bare rocks across a moorland. The wind blows against her billowing her shawl.

She picks a tiny flower from between the crevice of a rock.

EXTERIOR. ETNA. EARLY EVENING

Mount Etna rises majestically in the far distance through mountains and woods. The sky is sombre and darkening.

EXTERIOR. SUMMIT OF ETNA. EARLY DAWN.

From the summit the whole of Sicily, imbued with the shadows of an early dawn, is spread below the mountain slopes. The tranquil sea around the island is dusky and pearly.

EXTERIOR. ETNA. MID MORNING.

From the distance Mount Etna crowned with snow rises into a fresh crisp blue sky.

EXTERIOR. MARIA'S HOUSE. MORNING.

Maria is sweeping the street in front of her house with a straw brush. The dust coils up floating.

She sweeps along the street further and further. Her neighbours, on seeing her from their glass-fronted doors, recoil into their houses.

Assunta runs towards Maria and pulls her mother by the hand back towards the house.

ASSUNTA
Mamma! Mamma! Stop it!

Maria in recognition of Assunta's concern lets herself be led back towards home.

INTERIOR. MARIA'S HOUSE. BEDROOM. EVENING.

Maria is sitting in front of her dressing table staring emptily at her own reflection.

EXTERIOR. MARIA'S HOUSE. DAWN.

The first glimmer of dawn. Maria leaves her house, wrapped in a black shawl and carrying flowers.

EXTERIOR. STREET. DAWN.

Maria is walking along the winding streets lost in the loneliness of the empty village. We hear in the chill air the tingling of bells. Maria walks on unerringly.

EXTERIOR. VILLAGE STREET. DAWN.

Maria turns a corner when suddenly she is confronted by a large flock of sheep which, like a river soon after a heavy torrential rain, floods the street. Behind the sheep are two shepherds in black.

Maria feels blocked. She is immobilised almost in panic and throws her shoulders against the wall.

The sheep rush past her.

She stays with her back against the wall as the flock of sheep, like a swollen river, brush past her.

EXTERIOR. STREET. DAWN.

The tail end of the flock goes by. She continues to stand in terror against the wall, clutching her flowers to her bosom.

The shepherds waving their sticks, pass her by without acknowledgement.
The street is now empty and covered in droppings.

After a few moments Maria unfreezes herself and hesitantly steps forward to walk along the deserted streets of the village.

EXTERIOR. CEMETERY. GRAVESTONE. DAWN.

Maria places her flowers on the black marble grave.

She kneels at the headstone and kisses the photograph of her husband. Her breath clouds the glass of his image.

She takes the vase and removes the previous flowers placing them beside the fresh flowers.

She tips the water away into the ground.

EXTERIOR. CEMETERY. GRAVESTONE. DAWN.

Maria replaces the vase with fresh flowers and begins to polish the black marble.

Slowly her lone figure recedes amidst the graves and the tall cypress trees.

INTERIOR. CHURCH. MORNING.

Don Lillo celebrates the first morning Mass. From behind the altar he glances over the congregation looking for Maria.

The congregation consists of about half a dozen elderly women, some sitting in pairs, others scattered around the church.

An old peasant man dressed in heavy corduroy clothes kneels half hidden at the back.

Maria is not there.

INTERIOR. MARIA'S KITCHEN. DAY.

Maria is busy walking back and forth from the terrace to the kitchen, bringing in clothes.

Vincenzo, Assunta and Anna Maria are sitting around the table eating lunch.

An extra plate of food stands untouched.

> VINCENZO
> *Mamma, the food is getting cold.*

Maria continues folding clothes.

> ASSUNTA
> *Mamma, your food is getting cold.*

> ANNA MARIA
> *Mamma, you tell me*
> *that I must eat in order to grow,*
> *now you will stop growing if*
> *you don't eat.*

Maria smiles.

> MARIA
> *I'm already grown up.*
> *It's you who must grow.*

> VINCENZO
> *Come on now, come and sit down.*

Maria affectionately strokes Vincenzo's head.

MARIA
You Vincenzo think about passing your exams
and don't make a fuss about me.

INTERIOR. MARIA'S HOUSE. LATER.

Giuseppe and Vincenzo are seated at the table with books
strewn across it. They are revising together and making
notes.

Vincenzo puts down his pen.

VINCENZO
I can't concentrate.

GIUSEPPE
I know.

Giuseppe rises from his chair and moves to Vincenzo
who lets his head fall. Vincenzo affectionately places his
arm over Vincenzo's shoulders.

EXTERIOR. COUNTRY ROADS. LATE AFTERNOON.

Vincenzo holds onto Giuseppe as they ride together
on the Vespa through winding country roads.

EXTERIOR. ORCHARD. CISTERN. LATE AFTERNOON

Vincenzo and Giuseppe are swimming in the water.

Two towels lie spread out next to each other under the
mottled shade of a lemon tree.

EXTERIOR. ORCHARD BASIN. LATER.

Vincenzo and Giuseppe are lying face down on the towels.

EXTERIOR. CEMETERY. AVENUE. DAWN.

Maria walks alone through the darkened lonely avenue of cypress trees.

EXTERIOR. CEMETERY. GRAVESTONE. MORNING.

Maria is rearranging new flowers on the grave.

Her face is reflected in the black shiny marble.

Don Lillo stands above her with a disapproving look.

Maria turns anxiously to him.

> DON LILLO
> *Why don't you come to Mass?*

> MARIA
> *I don't feel that I want to be with people.*

> DON LILLO
> *Yesterday Carmela was asking about you.*
> *We are all concerned.*

> MARIA
> *What are people saying?*

> DON LILLO
> *Nobody is saying anything harmful.*
> *No one wants to see you so isolated*
> *from the rest of the village...*

Maria looks down.

> DON LILLO
> *A few times a week is enough to*
> *pay respect to your husband. Totò*
> *would want you to go on living.*
> *You are young and you have such lovely*
> *children to be proud of,*
> *the fruit of your marriage to Totò.*

Don Lillo puts his arm around Maria's shoulder and lifts her to her feet.

Maria casts a blank gaze towards Don Lillo's concerned eyes.

> DON LILLO
> *Come. Come let's walk together to the church.*

EXTERIOR. COUNTRYSIDE. DAWN.

Don Lillo walks with Maria through the countryside towards the village.

EXTERIOR. CHURCH. MORNING.

Maria and Don Lillo enter the church.

INTERIOR. VILLAGE CHURCH. MORNING.

Maria is sitting alone at the back of the church. A few scattered elderly parishioners make up the congregation.

Don Lillo, in ceremonial vestments, is celebrating Mass at the altar.

Maria, motionless, holds a rosary.

EXTERIOR. VILLAGE. WINTER.

Large flakes of snow are falling from the sky onto the snow-covered mountain village. Everything is white. The azure sea glistens in the distance.

EXTERIOR. MARIA'S HOUSE. DAY.

The black drapery over the door is now tattered and frayed.

EXTERIOR. VILLAGE. EARLY EVENING.

The village passeggiata.

Everyone in the village parades, looking their best.

Groups of pensioners in black caps sit outside their clubs watching the passing crowds and talk together.

Two men in their fifties walk side by side.

ROSARIO
Maria has changed so much.

VILLAGER
*May her husband's
soul rest in peace.*

ROSARIO
*He was a good man. A hard worker.
I never saw him drunk once.*

VILLAGER
*She has distanced herself from
everybody in the village.
She has sunk into herself.*

ROSARIO
She has become distant even from her own children,.
and she acts so strangely now with all
these dawn pilgrimages.

VILLAGER
Yes, a pity. She is still such a handsome woman.

EXTERIOR. STREET. DAY.

Maria comes out into the street. She walks into the middle of the street. As she proceeds along the street some of the neighbours retreat inside.

EXTERIOR. COUNTRYSIDE. NOVEMBER. SUNSET.

Maria wanders over the landscape as the sun sets.

She walks through fields covered with wild flowers.

EXTERIOR. COUNTRYSIDE. NOVEMBER. SUNSET.

Maria sits alone. She is an isolated figure in the landscape, looking at the sea in the distance.

EXTERIOR. CHURCH. SUNDAY MORNING.

The church bells ring out.

The villagers are converging on the church in their Sunday best.

INTERIOR. CHURCH. SUNDAY MORNING.

The small village church is bright with the November sunlight.

Beams of sunlight pierce through windows illuminating the altar.

A congregation fills up the small church.

Local dignitaries, including the Mayor, sit in the first two rows. People of all ages are at the Mass.

INTERIOR. CHURCH. LATER.

The Sunday Mass is in its later stages with Don Lillo standing at the white marble altar dressed in ceremonial robes. He is flanked by altar boys swinging thuribles of smoking incense in the air. Their metal chains clang faintly.

A child's cry echoes out inside the church.

Beams of sunlight which illuminate the marbled altar show dust particles in the air.

The congregation follows the ceremony intently.

Suddenly the main church doors fly open.
Maria in a black shawl storms into the church in a state of great nervous agitation and distress.

She walks fast and determinedly down the aisle towards the marble altar.

The congregation turns and looks at her in astonishment.

Don Lillo, immobilised, with frightened eyes and with a terrible presentiment within him, watches Maria as she strides towards the altar.

Maria walks up the altar steps and climbs onto the white marble knocking the gold chalice.

As the chalice falls down the marble steps a sharp metallic clang chillingly echoes out inside the church.

Maria stands on the altar and with desperate eyes stares out at the congregation.

She points towards them. Her shawl slides from her shoulders onto the ground.

She shouts out accusingly.

MARIA
You are all conspiring against me. I know it.
You all hate me.
You want my body.
All of you.

She swings round pointing to all of the congregation, sending a chill through everybody's heart.

Then slowly her arm comes to rest pointing at Don Lillo. She collapses sobbing onto the white marble altar.

Don Lillo lets his head fall.

Maria's trembling body lies splayed on the cold white marble of the altar; as a chill current darts through her entire body.

The whole congregation is in an uneasy shock as Maria sobs on the altar.

A beam of sunlight full of floating dust particles climbs away from her, up through a high window to the fresh blue November sky.

EXTERIOR. TERRACE. MORNING.

Clothes flap in the wind. Anna Maria and Assunta are skipping. Vincenzo is reading.

Maria, no longer dressed in black, is hanging out wet clothes taking them from a basket and pegging them on the line.

> MARIA
> (To the children)
> *Be careful of the pots.*

Maria's elderly mother is sitting on the terrace watching Maria approvingly.

EXTERIOR. MARIA'S HOUSE. VILLAGE. MORNING.

Maria leaves her house. The black drapery has gone. The black-edged paper with the words 'To my beloved husband' still remains pinned to the door.

Anna Maria clutches Maria's skirt. Assunta holds Maria's hand.

EXTERIOR. VILLAGE STREETS. MORNING.

Maria and the girls walk hand-in-hand through the busy village streets.

In the doorways and in the streets, villagers acknowledge Maria. Maria greets them in return.

EXTERIOR. FRONT OF SCHOOL. MORNING.

Maria kisses both Anna Maria and Assunta and smiles.

MARIA
(to Assunta)
Make sure Anna Maria eats her brioche during break.

ASSUNTA
Yes Mamma.

The girls run off into the school.

Maria exchanges pleasantries with the other parents.

INTERIOR. VILLAGE CHURCH. DAY

Maria is arranging flowers in the church with another woman. A second woman sweeps the church floor. A third polishes the wooden pews.

Don Lillo approaches the altar as the women continue their respective tasks.

He looks on Maria and her companion approvingly.

DON LILLO
*Maria, how beautifully you have
arranged the flowers.*

MARIA
Yes, they are beautiful flowers.

INTERIOR. MARIA'S HOUSE. KITCHEN. DAY.

A radio plays in the background.

Maria is helped by Anna Maria and Assunta as they prepare food for Anna Maria's birthday.

They decorate the birthday cake with coloured sweets. Little cakes are prepared and displayed on plates for the party.

Assunta slices vegetables.

A metal tray of lasagne is on the table.

INTERIOR. MARIA'S HOUSE. LIVING ROOM. EVENING.

The room is full of music. Relatives and friends are dancing to tangos and mazurkas, generally enjoying themselves. Some are singing.

INTERIOR. MARIA'S HOUSE. LIVING ROOM. EVENING.

Several girls dance with Anna Maria. At the edge of the dance older relatives look on, amused.

Maria fetches Anna Maria, taking her by the hand and leading her to the table where the sweets and the cake are displayed.
Anna Maria climbs on a chair and leans over towards the birthday cake decorated with lit candles.

Everyone comes to a stop and gathers around Anna Maria to watch.

GIRLS
Make a wish Anna Maria,
Make a wish...
Wishes last forever.

Anna Maria glances at her mother, knowing that Maria is happier. Then she closes her eyes and blows the candles out in several puffs.

All the guests cheer her.

GUESTS
(Singing in English)
Happy birthday to you, Happy birthday to you.

INTERIOR. MARIA'S HOUSE. LIVING ROOM. LATER.

The party is in full swing. Everyone is dancing.

EXTERIOR. VILLAGE. DAY.

A trader's van moves along the busy village streets calling out through a loudspeaker.

TRADER
Come. Come. Come and buy my wonderful
courgettes, artichokes, pears,
apples...

INTERIOR. VILLAGE. DAY.

The trader's van is stopped in the village street. The trader is selling his produce.

Maria together with other women is buying fruit and vegetables from the trader. The trader looks at Maria as he fills the bag.

TRADER
They are a delight,
my fruit is
so sweet and tender
that it melts in the mouth.

MARIA
(smiling tongue in cheek)
Oh yes? Really?

INTERIOR. MARIA'S HOUSE. AFTERNOON.

Vincenzo and Giuseppe are sitting side by side reading from their books, studying. Books and papers are scattered over the table. They jump up and leave.

EXTERIOR. COUNTRY ROADS. AFTERNOON

Vincenco and Giuseppe are riding together on the Vespa. Vincenzo has his arms around Giuseppe's waist and the right side of his face is resting on Giuseppe's back.

EXTERIOR. ORANGE GROVE. CISTERN. AFTERNOON

Vincenzo and Giuseppe, naked, dive into the water which reflects the oranges hanging heavily from the trees. The air is sweet with orange blossom. They play splashing in the water and they embrace.

EXTERIOR. ORANGE GROVE. AFTERNOON. LATER.

Vincenzo and Giuseppe lie naked together face down under the dappled shade of the orange tree with water glistening on their olive coloured bodies.

They rest their arms over each other's shoulders. They smile, their lips almost touching. They kiss each other.

The air is noisy with the buzzing of insects.

EXTERIOR.CEMETERY. AVENUE OF CYPRESSES. 9AM

It is All Soul's Day. An avenue of cypress trees lines the approach to the cemetery. Between the cypresses there are many flower vendors selling the most beautiful fresh chrysanthemums.

Their dazzling yellows, oranges and russets glow.

Some of the stalls have large clusters of dark mourning roses and branches from black-berried shrubs.

Other vendors sell black balloons for the children and varieties of seeds and nuts for the mourners to eat whilst they spend their whole day at the gravesides.

Crowds of mourners pass through the cypress avenue.

Women whose wounds of recent bereavement are still raw walk supported by relatives.

Some women are carrying baskets of food and goods for a graveside picnic.

The men are wearing their best Sunday suits and black ties. In the lapels of their jackets they have either a black button or a black silk stripe.

Some of the men carry portable radios. Snatches of sound are flicking through the air.

INTERIOR. MARIA'S HOUSE. LIVING ROOM. MORNING.

Maria is wearing black. She smartens Vincenzo, Assunta and Anna Maria who are all dressed in their best. Maria ties a black silk ribbon around Anna Maria's hair.

Maria adjusts Assunta's hat, which is circled with a black ribbon.

Maria puts a black velvet button in the lapel of Vincenzo's jacket.

EXTERIOR. CEMETERY. GRAVESIDE. MORNING.

The cemetery is dotted with clusters of mourners.

Each group is gathered by their respective gravesides with flowers.

In the background, music plays from radios.

Above them through the cypress trees, there are glimpses of a beautifully clear winter sky.

Maria sits by the edge of her husband's grave.

Vincenzo, Assunta and Anna Maria sit around in a crescent at the foot of the grave.

Maria's mother sits to one side of the headstone.

Don Lillo sits opposite Maria's mother on the other side of the headstone.

Baskets of food are resting on the ground.

DON LILLO
Later I must go to visit another
family who have lost their mother.
Then I must visit a few other graves.

MARIA
You will come back for lunch, won't you?

DON LILLO
Of course I will come back.

Anna Maria gets up and runs to Don Lillo, who puts her on his knees.

Maria arranges the mourning roses and twigs of the berried shrub and places a few chrysanthemums on the black marble grave.

Maria, momentarily in an absent state, fixes her gaze on her own reflection in the black marble.

EXTERIOR. AVENUE OF CYPRESS TREES. DAWN.

The cypress trees stand in grey ranks with their tops swaying in a slight morning wind.

In the loneliness of dawn a small figure in black walks from the far end of the the cypress avenue towards the cemetery gates.

The figure of Maria walks steadily forward as if in a trance.

She is covered in a black silky shawl and bears in her arms a large cluster of globed yellow chrysanthemums.

EXTERIOR. CEMETERY. GRAVESIDE. DAWN.

The cemetery feels solitary and empty. The birds are twittering in the air.

Mournful cypress trees stand between the graves.

Maria places the globed yellow chrysanthemums upon the black marble grave.

She kneels and kisses the photograph of her husband.

Her lips rest upon the photograph. Again, her warm breath clouds the glass.

She then arranges the chrysanthemums neatly around the edges of the black marble grave.

She stands by the grave, letting her silky black shawl slide down curling onto the ground.

Calmy, Maria starts to unbutton her black blouse.

She lets her blouse fall.

Amidst the darkly monumental presence of cypress trees which stand solitary between the graves Maria disrobes until she stands, a small naked figure, beside her husband's grave.

EXTERIOR. GRAVE. DAWN.

Maria quietly lies naked on the black marble grave with the globed yellow chrysanthemums neatly arranged around her body.

As she lies on the cold marble of the grave, an icy current darts through her naked body which ruffles the smoothness of her flesh.

Absently, and in an empty state of mind, she gazes up at the sky.

EXTERIOR. GRAVE. (FROM THE AIR). MORNING.

Maria's naked figure lying on the black marble grave amidst the glowing yellow chrysanthemums, slowly becomes ever distant.

The opening sounds of Mozart's Requiem Mass are heard and move slowly to a crescendo, gradually filling the whole landscape.

The solitary, dark and monumental cypress trees emerge from between the graves reaching up into the clear sky. A light wind causes the tops of cypresses to sway gently.

The whole atmosphere is now impregnated with the sounds of Mozart's Requiem Mass.

The music lingers, then quietens, then rises — creating an almost unbearable melancholy beauty filled with light.

Then the music slowly quietens again and the scene fades into...

EXTERIOR. SICILIAN HILLSIDE. EARLY MORNING.

An almond tree, newly blossomed, stands on a breezy hillside bathed in the bright, soft Sicilian sunlight.

The blossom on the almond tree quivers with the breeze.
Gusts of wind move the blossoms on the branches.

A stronger gust of wind blows the petals up into the
fresh, blue, November sky.

*

Acknowledgements

*

During the writing of these pieces, over many years, many people have offered their kind advice and encouragement. I am extremely grateful to all of them for their support. In particular I would like to thank Professor Michael Worton of University College, London, who made many useful suggestions. The late Sir Isaiah Berlin during our many meetings at the Athenaeum Club and at the Richoux café in Piccadilly offered considerable encouragement. I also thank Professor J.S. Cummins, Professor Barbara Hardy, Desmond Hogan, the late Charles Montieth, the late John Morley, James Purdy, the late Sir Stephen Spender and Gore Vidal.

The story "Maria's Chrysanthemums" was first broadcast on Radio 3 during the 1990 BBC Promenade Concerts. I want to thank the producer, John Tydeman, and the reader, Robert Rietty, for their work. The first draft of the screenplay was written with the professional help of Paul Gallagher, a teacher of screenwriting. It is now intended, however, to stand as a literary work in its own right. I also thank Simon Callow and Mark Shivas (then of BBC Film) who offered words of encouragement.

"My Religion" (which inspired Francis King to write his novella, *Secret Lives)* was read by me between two movements of Bach's unaccompanied Cello Suites, in Saint James' Church, Piccadilly during a BBC memorial service for my beloved friend, Anthony Jennings (formerly of the BBC). He has also greatly influenced this book and it is dedicated to his memory.

Several of the stories and a few of the poems were first published in *The European Gay Review*.

*

About the author

*

Salvatore Santagati was born in Italy and educated in
Sicily, Milan and London. He studied philosophy at
University College, London.
He then went on to the London School of Economics
(LSE) where he completed a PhD on the German thinker,
Max Stirner.
His thesis was supervised by the late Sir Isaiah Berlin
with whom he also discussed literature.
Between 1986 and 1992 he edited the literary journal,
The European Gay Review, where he published many
distinguished writers.
He has also worked for the Institute of Contemporary
Arts, taught part-time at the LSE, translated into English
a short play by Dario Fo and was a regular contributor to
The Times Higher Educational Supplement.

He divides his time between London and Italy and travels
extensively.

*

A First Spring in Sicily

by

Salvatore Santagati

First published 2003 in
The European Union

by

Almond Grove Press
London
UK

© Salvatore Santagati 2003

*

Worldwide Distribution
and
Representation:

Central Books Ltd
99 Wallis Road
London E9 5LN

Telephone: 44 (0) 845 458 99 11

Fax: 44 (0) 845 458 99 12

email mo @ centralbooks.com.

Website: www.centralbooks.co.uk

*

Printed in England on acid-free paper.